# GOLF

## YOUR WAY

THOMAS SLAGLE

aventine press

This book is gratefully dedicated to the king of golf, Mr. Arnold Palmer, and the King of the Universe, the Lord Jesus Christ. I also want to acknowledge the loving patience of my beautiful wife Lisa and the assistance of my good friend and fellow journeyman, Bryant Creel, for his careful editing.


First Edition



Published by Aventine Press
55 East Emerson St.
Chula Vista CA, 91911
www.aventinepress.com

ISBN: 978-1-59330-938-1

# TABLE OF CONTENTS

# FORWARD

## CAN GOLF REALLY BE TAUGHT, OR ONLY LEARNED?

In recent years I have come to the realization that the golf swing cannot be taught to me, only learned by me. I think this principle applies not only to my own efforts, but to those of many, many other golfers — possibly even all others. It makes golf, in my opinion, virtually impossible to teach. Teachers are being asked to teach something that, if they are completely honest about it, they do not understand and may very well be learning about each and every day that they delve into its mysteries. Normally the student believes that there is a secret, or method, or drill, or learning that will increase their skill in the game much more quickly. I believe that if there is such a system, it is unique to that person and in the overwhelming number of cases lies in simplicity rather than complexity.

No golf "system or method" works for anybody or everybody all the time. Anyone who even suggests that they know or have even a remote perception as to what the best golf swing is for you is either deluded or arrogant. No one on this earth completely understands what's going on in the golf swing any more than in virtually all of the rest of life. It's that subtle and complicated (and that wonderful). I believe that if golf instructors, teachers, so-called experts (myself included) actually knew anything special about the golf swing and had to tell the truth about the golf swing a decent golf lesson would look something like this:

> Student: "What's the best way to grip the club [or stand up to it, lag it, plane it, loop it, find my right tempo, or whatever]?"

> Old Expert: "Well, it's funny. Most of it depends on the person. A whole lot of different things work for a lot of different people. But something that works for everybody - all the time? I have been searching my whole life and I haven't been able to figure that one out. A lot of other guys spent their whole lives looking for it and never found anything that worked for very long either. Sometimes you stumble across something - some swing image, almost always just a feeling, lot of times hard to describe to others because of the limitations of human language. It might work for a week, conceivably even a month, assuming you are beating those balls every day like "working" instead of "playing" golf. Then it all falls apart and the next day you've got to start looking again. Funny thing, sometimes the best ideas might come from the weirdest places – like overhearing one thirty-six handicapper tell the other thirty-six what he was thinking about when he hit his best shot. Sometimes the method guys' stuff works for some people for a while – weird thing is, it seems sometimes to work best for those people who seem to be able to convince themselves that their "system" really is superior – maybe that Leadbetter/Faldo burst a few years back was like that. But most times a few bad shots turn up and they start to question their "system"; so they start looking at somebody else's "system." Maybe that is a little bit of what Mr. Tiger's going through. Plus, maybe like they say, injuries caused from snapping that lead leg like that. But you have got

to admire his tenacity – he is back out there looking, digging, hoping for something. Something like heaven maybe. Maybe they are all looking and digging in the wrong place."

Student: "What about this Hogan guy? I looked on Amazon and it seems like everybody that ever wrote a golf book, and there are a gazillion of them, has some insight into the secret of golf, or what you just referred to as heaven, and bunches of them talk about Mr. Hogan. He is always referred to as Mr. Hogan, out of reverence I guess. He sold the "secret" to some magazine in the fifties for what was then a huge sum of money. What do you think about this Mr. Hogan?"

Old Expert: "You know Mr. Hogan stumps me too. A couple of very strange things; you might have heard that he put that extra spike in one of his shoes, can't remember which one right now. Had to send the shoe off to England to have it done."

Student: "That is odd, and why England? Maybe if he thought it helped his swing, it did help."

Old Expert: "You may be on to something there. You know, I learned my first fundamentals of golf from his Five Lessons book from the fifties. But eventually it quit working for me and I started looking elsewhere. But the last fifteen years or so, like a lot of people, I have been looking at a lot of video of Mr. Hogan at different times in his career, and guess what? As far as I can tell he never swung in real life like he said he did in the book. Of course the book only has pencil drawings. It seems like he was like just about everybody I see swing a golf club – his golf swing evolved throughout his life."

Student: "You know that horrible accident he had with that bus that crippled him and he played some of the best golf ever played on earth after that – people say it was some kind of a miracle. What's your take?"

Old Expert: "Well, I am not much on religion, so I'll have to ponder that one a bit and get back to you."

Student: "Hey, I've got one more question. I have a twelve-year-old who wants to take up golf. If you could tell her what you would want to know if you could start all over again, what would you want her to know?"

Old Expert: "Well, that's easy. I would want her to have this book you are about to read, and tell her to enjoy every moment of an incredible journey. In a perfect world (some might call it heaven) we play golf (and the golf swing for that matter), not work at it."

# INTRODUCTION

Inspired by Arnold Palmer I started playing golf at the age of twelve. A crusty old golf pro taught me the standard Vardon grip and a square stance. I was hooked from the first instant that my old Sam Snead Blue Ridge seven-iron met an old x-ed out Club Special range ball that inevitably pull-sliced sharply. Despite my best efforts that ugly shot shape continued repeatedly for a half-hour whenever the contact was solid enough. But I wasn't too worried. Surely that problem could be fixed easily with the right expert instruction and I could grasp everything that needed to be known about the golf swing and how to play great golf. As I imagine you have gathered by now I was wrong. I was completely, utterly dead wrong.

I was a smart, inquisitive kid, so I sought the answers in a logical place – books. I went to the base library on the military base where my father was stationed and located and checked out two books: The first was Five Lessons: The Modern Fundamentals of Golf by Ben Hogan. If you are reading the present book, you are no doubt familiar with it: revered, admired, you might say even worshipped — even today the gold standard of golf instruction. I refer to it as the bible of golf instruction, and it is by far the best-selling and most referred to sports instruction manual of all time. How could a serious student go wrong with it?

The second book was much more obscure — way much more. Five Simple Steps to Perfect Golf was by a character who called himself Count Yogi. You read that correctly. Count Yogi. Inside were pictures of the Count: in one he wore striped parachute pants, a cape, a billowy shirt, rings on every finger and a turban. The Count did everything, including his golf swing, "the Count's way." This "Count" made ridiculous claims – that he was the greatest golfer that ever lived (in spite of never practicing), that he never took a practice swing and, most astonishingly, that he was blackballed from playing the PGA tour because his play was so superior that it would embarrass the other pros. Yogi's book was amusing but, needless to say, I was much more inclined to go with the staid Mr. Hogan. But, there was one thing that put the final nail in the coffin of Yogi's book for me. From the pictures inside you could tell that Yogi had a long, flowing, graceful swing but at impact he had a cupped left wrist. The club head looked like it was actually ahead of his hands, and he did it on every shot from the driver through the putter. The Count was a flipper! The Greatest Golfer of all time was a fraud – a hacker. He had to be if he flipped it.

Even at twelve I knew that was wrong. Even then I knew about the flat left wrist. I had seen the pictures in Five Lessons of Mr. Hogan's left wrist at impact. It was slightly arched. Surely that was a fundamental that would have to be included in any fundamentally sound golf swing. I was wrong, and as I look back on it now, I realize, frighteningly wrong. After more than a half-century of study, research, lessons, beating millions (okay, tens of thousands anyway) of balls, anguish, and frustration, I realize that Mr. Hogan's left wrist position at impact was in no way superior to or inferior to the Count's position. They are simply different, but equally capable of producing great, even perfect golf shots if left to the control of the player's subconscious mind. Logically, I chose Mr. Hogan's book to be the blueprint for my golf swing and forgot for many years about the ridiculous Count.

I began to eat, sleep, and breathe Five Lessons. I got the grip cold. I still have the same grip today. It is completely ingrained. It feels horrible to hold the club any other way. I got the posture cold. I was sitting on the spectator stick. I was under the pane of glass. I had the foot positions and ball positions from the back of the book cold. I could feel the big rubber band pull my left hip around to start the downswing. If there was any justice in golf, I should have hit nothing but Hogan power fades. But guess what? I hit nothing but pull slices for a year. What was I doing wrong? I would reread Mr. Hogan. I must have missed something.

Eventually I moved on from Mr. Hogan to other swing theories. I assumed, like almost everybody, that there was some secret, some theory, some set of fundamentals, some technique that applied to me, or even everybody, that could open up the door to great ball-striking. Lots of people who play golf have theories about how to play golf – from every thirty-six handicapper to the best players in the world and their acclaimed instructors – most assume that their own theories are superior to others. In my humble opinion they are not – they are all equally valid and equally invalid. All are helpful to somebody and none applies to everybody, or even most people. That is simply the nature of this incomprehensible game.

After fifty years of study, practice and frustration, I have come up with some guiding principles that have helped me become satisfied with own my golf swing. Will they help you? I don't know. I think so, but I can only know what is within my own experience. I summarize those idea as follows:

- No one can teach you golf, you can only teach yourself.
- The golf swing cannot be completely understood, never has been, and never will be; it is like everything in life, far too complex.
- There are no fundamentals of the golf swing (i.e., requirements that every golfer must meet to have a workable swing) (in my opinion, the ball flight laws, the only thing that really matters in achieving the results that we seek, are not swing

fundamentals, but simply laws of physics that are essential for us to know and obey if we are to be successful).

- No serious golf swing system or set of fundamentals that I'm familiar with is superior to or inferior to any other system (they are all workable but dangerous to your progress as a golfer if you believe they are superior).
- Your golf swing evolves every day of your life and will continue to do so every day that you play.
- The golf swing is controlled by your subconscious mind and excessive interference by your conscious mind inhibits its ability to carry out its goal of striking the ball out of the club face sweet spot with the correct club path and club face alignment.
- Many of the greatest ball-strikers share two things in common:
  a. - they were great experimenters (they were not afraid to try their own often radical swing thoughts); and
  b. - they hit massive numbers of practice balls (feeding their subconscious minds' ability to achieve its goal).

I did not realize these things until after I was sixty. However, once I realized them it miraculously changed my ball-striking and my golf game. Today, my irons are crisper and straighter than they've ever been. My driver carry distance is the longest it is ever been (at sixty-four years old). I chip better and I putt better; and not just a little better, but much better.

The best thing about it is that I no longer rely on anyone else's swing fundamentals. On most days the only swing thought that I use is to bounce the ball off the sweet spot with the appropriate club path and club face angle. I have found that I am free to actually play golf and create golf shots for the first time in my life. Will a similar approach work for you? I don't know. It might. It will not hurt to try before jumping into the next new swing theory. If it does nothing else, it might convince you that almost always you are your own best teacher both in golf and in life.

# CHAPTER 1.

## HOW MINDY BLAKE WAS WRONG

An Englishman named Mindy Blake wrote two books in the seventies describing a golf swing technique that he claimed to have developed and used. I think he was a scientist of some type. I am not sure but I believe he was a pretty good golfer. The titles of his books intrigued me: The Golf Swing of the Future and Golf, The Technique Barrier. I thought: finally here was the key to the kingdom - once it was unlocked great golf was finally here for everybody.

I tried Blake's techniques on two occasions - once in the seventies and once in the nineties, both times for a long enough period of time (at least a month or two) to ensure that I understood and used the technique as described. I will not describe his technique in full, but a brief description would be a decidedly open stance (even more than Lee Trevino's) with a forty-five degree open left foot flare and a very strong four-knuckled grip. As I recall, the club was moved straight backwards in the backswing. A full description can easily be found if the reader will google the Alternative Swing Theory forum on the internet.

To my mind, Blake's theory did two things:

- The body and the foot position ensured that the lower body started the downswing (a good thing, isn't it?); and

- The four-knuckled grip required that the closing of the club face had to somehow be held off through impact to prevent the ball from starting left.

On both occasions my experimentation with Blake's theory produced the same result – my ball-striking got neither better nor worse. Blake's theory was not the future for me. It did not do the main thing that I needed at the time to help my own golf swing — a five mile per hour bump in club head speed (particularly with the driver). So, on both occasions I moved on to other theories that promised a little bump in power (maybe David Leadbetter's dog-wags-the-tail theory could deliver, or maybe I had missed something in Five Lessons).

What I now find fascinating about Blake's books are not his unique, and, to my mind, somewhat odd technique, but the underlying premise that he started from — that in golf there is a technique barrier. Blake reasoned, and it made a lot of sense to me, that in sports there are "technique barriers"; techniques, or fundamental methods of movement, if you will, that, once understood and mastered, could unlock new levels of sports performance. He believed that these techniques applied to everybody, and in golf would improve everybody's game. The example that Blake used, and I think it was a wonderful one, was of Dick Fosbury and the high jump. When I was in high school in the sixties the technique for the high jump was to go over the bar forward. Every high jumper did it: professional, amateur, college, high school, whoever. Suddenly Dick Fosbury comes out of nowhere and starts doing the unthinkable (at least at that time) and starts jumping over backwards! And breaking records! Within five years every world class high jumper was doing the "Fosbury flop" and records began to drop everywhere at a rate far quicker than ever before. Within ten years you couldn't find a high jumper anywhere going over the bar forwards. Today going over the bar forwards is virtually nonexistent in competition.

Blake reasoned that the golf swing was like the high jump (and other sports) in that it was subject to technique barriers that once recognized and analyzed, could allow the creation of novel techniques that could create incremental, or even massive jumps in performance. He believed, I assume, that his theory of the golf swing was a theory that was one of these barrier breakers. I assume he believed that once his theory was publicly available, some physically gifted player would adopt it and achieve great success. That would lead to its adoption by other players, more success and eventually the Blake theory would be the new gold standard of golf instruction (who knows, maybe replacing Five Lessons).

We all know that this hasn't happened and more than fifty years have passed. His books are no doubt out of circulation and I know of no world class ball-striker that uses fundamentals remotely close to Blake's. The closest would in my opinion be Lee Trevino but I am fairly certain that Lee Trevino never read Blake's books and, if he had, would not have blindly followed the instruction. Trevino was completely self-taught (in my opinion the absolute best way to be) and once famously said, "I would never take a golf lesson from anybody who couldn't beat me." That principle must have narrowed the field of his potential golf instructors considerably. I think I can say with certainty that Lee Trevino mastered the ability to smash the ball right out of the sweet spot of the club face with the correct club path and club face angles (which is the only thing that really physically matters) with much greater frequency than Blake ever did with his "technique."

It is no doubt unfair to compare Blake to Trevino but I cannot help but wonder what was different about the two of them that might account for the difference in what they achieved in mastering ball-striking. After all, they were both inordinately interested in the subject. Blake wrote two books on the subject and I doubt that they were ghost-written as I imagine Lee's golf instruction book may have been. I am speculating, but I will list several factors that could have played a part (listed in the order of importance, in my opinion):

- Lee probably hit more golf balls than Mindy (practice and play) during his golf swing's formative years - most likely many times more. Thus he had much more training of his subconscious mind to learn to accomplish the assigned task.
- Lee's innate talent (mainly hand-eye coordination, but also strength, stamina and flexibility) and resulting skill development was probably higher;
- Lee's desire for success may have been higher, possibly much higher; and
- Lee may have experimented more often, using different and unique swings thoughts that may have enhanced his subconscious mind's ability to obtain the necessary results.

In reality these factors could be listed in any order, even reversed, and might be equally meaningful. It's another one of those things that I don't know and that no one knows or could ever know. It is just another of those many things which are too complex for human understanding. But I believe it helps to at least think about such things because doing so helps us to consciously understand the process of motor learning. I believe understanding that process improves subconscious learning. I do not know why – I just know it appears that it has helped me. Give it a try. It might work for you too. The worst thing that can happen is that does not work for you.

The thing that interests me most about Blake is that his books describe most clearly what almost all of us think — that there is some barrier or "secret" about the golf swing that if discovered and applied properly can help us learn to strike the ball easily and purely. Of course, the most famous secret in golf instruction is "Hogan's secret" which he claimed to have in the fifties and has been debated ad nauseam ever since. I will not try to recount the different theories about Hogan's secret, but I will tell you, for what they are worth, my own ideas about those secrets. First, there are probably different kinds of "golf secrets." There are those that might be very specific to a particular player at a particular time in his own golf swing evolution — say Hogan in the summer of 1955. It might be a barrier breaker for him, but totally worthless or even harmful to the golf swings of others. That may be the kind of secret he was talking about. Another type of secret it could be is one that was a barrier breaker for him and might be a barrier breaker for other skilled ball-strikers (i.e., his professional competition). I think that may be how he viewed his secret given his competitive nature. Also, there could be a "secret" that could be a barrier breaker for all golfers, or at least those willing to put in a little work to ingrain it. I think that is the least likely alternative since no other of the millions of golfers over the last five hundred years has apparently come up with it.

Whenever I hear something about Hogan's secret it conjures up in my mind some very negative ideas about Hogan. I apologize if you are a fervent fan of his. But one of the things I've noticed about almost all of those who share our addiction to this horrible ( I am only half-kidding), frustrating game is that they are generous with their help to other addicts. I am not a very altruistic person but I do know that when I make a significant discovery about my own swing, I share it gladly with friends or just acquaintances who suffer with their own swings. It might help them too.

But, lets return to Hogan and his "secret." Imagine you are recognized as one of the greatest golfers of all time and are almost universally recognized as the greatest ball-striker of all time. You reach the height of the professional golf world. You spend virtually your entire life "digging the secret out of the dirt." You know that there are millions of others out there on the same frustrating journey. Then you find it! The secret of golf! You found a key that can unlock a joyful golf game for everybody. What do you do with the secret? Give it to your best friend? Give it to those you know who struggle the most? Give it to the world? Keep it quiet until you retire from competition, then give it to the world? How about let everybody know that you have got the secret but you will not tell? How about profit from books and magazine articles on golf instruction, but not divulge the true secret? How about teasing them with: "Well, it's there if you know where to look." How about taking it with you the grave? I like to think that the real Mr. Hogan was not like that but that is the impression I get from the accounts I have heard. Hopefully, I have only heard the wrong accounts. But, in my opinion, someone in Mr. Hogan's position who truly had the secret of golf, a treasure which might benefit millions of golfers, and took it to his grave, would be a cruel miser indeed.

It's just my opinion, but if Hogan had a secret it was in his statement that if you wanted it, you would have to "dig it out of the ground." But that's not a secret — that is something we all secretly know if we are willing to admit it. The four greatest pure ball-strikers in my lifetime are in my opinion Hogan, Moe Norman, Lee Trevino, and George Knudson. I think it is no coincidence that, based on all accounts, those same four individuals hit more practice balls than any other individuals who ever lived. If you know of any person who hit more balls than any one of those four please let me know. The volume of training of their subconscious mind's ability to direct their bodies to smash the ball right out of the center of the club face time after time was unparalleled. Add to that the mirror work and slow motion training they did. They were obsessed with the full golf swing. It is also interesting to me that none of the four were consistently great putters. I would guess that if any of the four had spent more time improving their green reading and visualization skills, and training putting touch their scores would have been even lower.

Especially with respect to Moe Norman, the number of practice balls they hit in their lifetimes is simply superhuman. We hear that sometimes he hit over two thousand balls in a day. I am not talking about chips and pitches or half-wedges but sometimes full-blooded irons, fairway woods and drivers. When I was in my twenties and fit, I sometimes hit six or seven hundred full shots in a day. It would take me all day and it was exhausting. My muscles would ache, my hands would be sore and I would pay for it the next day. I never had the will, desire or endurance to repeat it a second day. Based on my experiences, hitting over two thousand shots a day for many days, for a more than sixty year period is not only an incredible feat of superhuman strength and endurance but is also an amazing example of single-minded determination perhaps unmatched in any field of human endeavor. With all due respect to those who try to minutely copy Moe's unique physical swing and mannerisms, I suggest Moe would have become have an unbelievable ball-striker assuming any sensible and simple technique he adopted as long as he did not override his subconscious mind's innate ability to develop incredibly precise hand-eye coordination. The only way I can think of that might really disturb that miraculous system would be to try to reboot it with an entirely new swing method every time he had a bad day or hit some inevitable bad shots. I know, I've been there too many times.

Perhaps the most interesting thing about Mindy Blake and his technique barrier theory is to consider what is fundamentally different about high jumping and striking a golf ball. Why would one be subject to a technique barrier (as high jumping obviously was) and the other not? I have given it considerable thought and all I can come up with is that golf ball-striking is fundamentally involves more hand-eye coordination than high jumping and that somehow permits a much greater number of techniques to work equally well or close to equally well. I mentioned the high jumping/golf swing dichotomy to my dentist who is an avid golfer also. He suggested that perhaps by the fifties all the major technique barriers had been already breeched in golf. I think that is an interesting idea but still does not explain the success of out-of-the-box techniques such as those employed Lee Trevino, Calvin Peete or Jim Furyk.

So what can we learn from thinking about Blake's technique theory? For me, Blake's technique (or group of fundamentals) was not any better or any worse than any other system I have experimented with over the years which includes, **inter alia**, the following:

- Hogan's ideas both from Five Lessons (numerous times) and from Power Golf; Moe Norman or Natural Golf and its several incarnations; Jim Hardy, both one-plane and two-plane; Jimmy Ballard (connection system); Square-to-Square (both the 1970's and 2000's variations); David Leadbetter's dog-wags-the-tail and The A Swing; Lee Trevino; Joe Dante's "Four Magic Moves"; Gary Edwin's "Right-Sided Swing"; Mike Malaska (from YouTube); Annika Sörenstam; Mickey Wright; Sam Snead; George Knudson's "Natural Golf Swing"; Byron Nelson; Jim McLean; Arnold Palmer; Butch Harmon; Rick Smith; my own "Economical Golf Swing"; Hank Haney; Martin Ayers (from YouTube); and Homer Kelly (several variations of the alternatives he catalogs in The Golfing Machine). I don't know how many other "systems" I have experimented with (many are lost in the fog of my memory). My best guess is I've mentioned maybe a third of the total.

I am not mentioning these to brag in any way about the extent of my "knowledge" or experience. The overwhelming majority of it is worthless knowledge. It is actually very embarrassing to me that I have never overcome my overwhelming obsession to uncover the "secret" of the golf swing. Several years ago I moved and gave away more than five hundred golf instruction books. I am embarrassed to say that there were about twenty-five I could not bear to part with (including Five Lessons) and that the collection has started to grow again. I cannot help it; it's a sickness. I greatly fear that I have wasted a tremendous amount of thought and practice time on systems that lead nowhere. You may have a similar obsession though hopefully not as severe. One of my purposes in writing this book is to maybe help cure someone else with a similar obsession.

To summarize, I have heard that Blake believed that golf was 100% technique. I could not disagree more. I have come to believe that on full shots golf is 95% (or more) hand-eye co-ordination [to make sure there is no confusion, when I refer to hand-eye coordination I am referring to the subconscious mind's ability to coordinate all of our body motions to strike the ball, not just the use of the hands] and the rest technique (and that technique is based mainly on feel rather than body positions). With regard to short game (chipping and pitching) I believe it is 99% hand-eye coordination and 1% technique (I will explain in a chapter on those shots). With regard to putting I believe it is 100% hand-eye coordination (I will explain in a chapter on putting). Hand-eye coordination is controlled by our subconscious minds, trained by experimentation and repetition; only well-trained by lots of repetition. As I have said, it is not surprising that Moe Norman, Ben Hogan, Lee Trevino and George Knudson hit it so much purer than their peers, or you and me. They had a lot more repetitions.

But, before you start training your hand-eye coordination there are a few absolute facts that you need to understand -- the ball flight laws. You have to understand exactly what you need to do with the club face and club path in order to get the results you want. They are the two things that are most essential to the impact conditions in the golf swing and are the subject of the two following chapters. In one sense we now have a great advantage on the the four great ball-strikers that I mentioned above — we now have absolutely accurate scientific data to show us precisely the perfect impact dynamics we need to obtain the ball flight characteristics we desire. That information may speed the development of the skills necessary to hone our ball-striking enormously if we will understand it completely and make full use of its consequences in developing our own personal swing fundamentals. Armed with this revolutionary knowledge we may not have to hit quite as many golf balls as Moe Norman did.

# CHAPTER 2

## HOW TO USE TRACKMAN FACTS RATHER THAN THEORY AND SPECULATION TO REDESIGN YOUR OWN FULL SWING – THE SEARCH MAY BE FINALLY OVER

When I refer to trackman in this book I am not referring to the actual Trackman Launch Monitor. I am referring to the actual scientific, verifiable data that we have learned though the use of that particular machine and other launch monitors (i.e., Flight Scope) since that data started to become generally available in the nineties. I have gotten most of my underlying information through the very helpful videos of a golf professional named Joseph Mayo who goes by the name Trackman Maestro on YouTube. Even if you think you are the biggest "feel" player in the history of golf, please look at this material and let it soak into your subconscious mind where it can be put to good use. I call it trackman information because as far I can tell that is what golf professionals, instructors and other players normally call it. Some (i.e., Bennett and Plummer, the Stack & Tilt swing originators) call it the ball flight laws. I actually prefer the term ball flight laws because it is so descriptive of the information these laws provide us. I fully believe that the understanding of these laws will prove to be the biggest revolution in the history of golf and golf instruction (past, present or future). For the first time in the history of golf we have laws – actual provable, verifiable scientific principles that apply to every golf ball that has ever been hit. We now know (not guess, assume, speculate, feel, or wonder about) why the ball goes where it goes.

Prior to the arrival of the trackman information what we knew about the ball flight that resulted from the collision of a round ball and a flat (but sometimes slightly curved) striking surface from a virtually unlimited number of angles was extremely limited. The possible potential ball flights resulting from such collisions are, after all, unlimited. It could be, to say the least, bewildering. Sure, we knew, or thought we knew, a few general things that generally held true through our observation and experience. The laws of trajectory were pretty obvious. To hit it higher we had to "launch" it higher. Nobody talked about "launch angle" but it was obvious that hitting it high was easy if the hands were farther behind relative to the club head at impact. Obviously, it's easier to hit it higher with a forward ball position. Nobody should need an expert golf instructor to tell them that and a twelve-year-old figures it out in his backyard in fifteen minutes with a seven-iron and a whiffle ball. The same is true with hitting it lower – you can move the ball back and the hands forward. I'm sorry, I don't mean to insult anybody, but if you need golf instruction on those concepts, you may lack the common sense necessary to ever be a good ball-striker or maybe you never took the time to think about it. I think it's that obvious.

Other things about trajectory were not as obvious but were learned pretty quickly by observation. If we caught the ball lower in the face it flew lower (usually, but not always) and if we caught it higher on the face it flew higher (always). Another thing was pretty intuitive. The ball goes further when we hit it on the sweet spot (they give it a name today – smash factor). I have never heard of a swing theory where sweet spot contact was not recommended (the only exceptions are what I would call specialty shots). There were a few things that we observed about mishits (which I like to refer to as anything where the club face strikes the ball significantly away from the sweet spot). If we missed out on the toe, a lot of times (not always) we would get a less powerful "toe hook." If we missed it on the heel side we would normally get a weaker fade. The ball flight laws now explain why this occurs.

But the place where the ball flight laws were completely misunderstood was with respect to sideways movement of the ball in the air (hooks, slices, draws, fades) - why it started on the line it did, curved in the direction it did, and perhaps, most importantly, how much it curved. As far as I can tell, prior to trackman, every good ball-striker in the world controlled this side spin subconsciously. [Joseph Mayo contends, I believe, that with respect to flying golf balls there are no "side spins", only backspin on a tilted axis. I defer to his knowledge on this, but will refer to this movement as side spin for ease of understanding].

The only theory of shot-shaping that I was ever taught, or anyone else for that matter, was the same one that was made famous by Jack Nicklaus in Golf My Way. Everybody knew that the side motions are governed primarily by some combination of swing path and club face angle. I believe that knowledge is common sense and may even be instinctive. The problem was not in creating the direction of the spin. The problem was getting the starting line exactly right and in controlling the severity of the curve. But logically we wanted rules to explain the starting direction and severity of curve – I don't know if it was Old Tom Morris, or Bobby Jones or Jack Grout who came up with the "logical" rule, but Mr. Nicklaus set it out most clearly in Golf My Way – he aimed his body ( assumed to control club path) where he wanted the ball to start and his club face where he wanted the ball to finish (the target). Logically it makes perfect sense. As we now know, if Jack did exactly as he planned to hit a draw (let's assume sweet spot contact and a flat lie) then that ball goes left of the target every time (it over curves). If a considerable amount of curve is being played for then that ball goes well left. If you combine that with the major issue of club face alignment at address that is considered in the following chapter ( we are normally taught to set the leading edge perpendicular to the target line) then the ball goes even further left. Not just sometimes, but always.

I tried the Nicklaus shot shaping technique - I thought everybody did. It was so logical: but no matter what I did the ball started left of the intended starting line and usually went further left of the target. I got advice from pros and friends and they watched the ball flight and said something like, "you came over the top." I now know that that observation was totally ridiculous and they were as bewildered as I was. No one ever suggested to me the blazingly simple notion that maybe that starting line was right where the face was pointing when the ball left the face and that with a simple adjustment of how I set the club face behind the ball (just a touch open) the ball would start on the proper line and draw (not fade!) right back to the target with the same swing that on the previous ball had resulted in the pull hook. My reaction to "the lefts" (as I called them) had always been to think something in my technique was wrong ( maybe I needed to reread Five Lessons) or maybe a new technique would solve it (enter Mindy Blake and all the others). Little did I know that the answer was science (but science that didn't exist at the time).

At first when I heard about trackman, I wasn't that impressed. I heard a lot of talk about tour guys trying to "zero out their numbers." Big deal, I thought, if I move the club head straight back and through and drive that ball right out of the sweet spot with the right launch angle at the same club head speed every time, the ball would go very straight and consistent. It was interesting but not very earth-shattering. Then I heard about the trackman data exploding the Nicklaus shot-shaping theory. For me it was earth-shattering. It convinced me of the unspeakable power of the subconscious mind and the importance it plays in golf. Nicklaus obviously hit lots of shots that curved right to his target from both directions. How did he do it with obvious flaws in his conscious ideas about shot shape? His subconscious mind did it (we might also say he used feel) through methods we can't even consciously fathom. Maybe his subconscious mind set that blade open or closed just the right amount at address. Maybe it held off the rotation of the toe past the heel just before impact, just a microsecond. Maybe it was some weird combination of multiple factors. We will never know. He will never know.

So, what are the shot-shaping laws of trackman? I have dumbed them down for my own use as I am not technically oriented. These are the ideas I actually use. To curve a ball to a target ( assume sweet spot contact) the club path should be twice the amount the club face is open or closed to the target line. I will give you the examples that I use. For a baby draw (for me) the path of the club should be two degrees in-to-out and the face should be one degree open to the target line. That ball will start out pretty straight down the face line because the face determines approximately eighty percent of the ball's starting direction. To me it still sounds illogical but we know it to be true and it works that way in reality. That two-to-one relationship holds up when playing larger curves (not exactly, but close enough that I don't think we need to worry about it). Anyway, for a slightly bigger draw, I go with four degrees in-to-out for the path and two degrees open to the target line for the face (again, open-faced draws). For a big draw I go to eight degrees in-to-out path and four degrees open to the target line face – a big looping hook out of an open face. I know it is inexact but it is based on physics and it works well for me.

Anyway, fades are just the opposite. For a baby fade (for me) path is two degrees out-to-in and club face one degree closed to target line (the close-faced fade – to me again it seemed counterintuitive, but it works). For a little bigger fade I go with four degrees out-to-in path and two degrees closed to the target line face. I do not go to the eight/four ratio if I want to big slice. I just go with a four/two and try to catch the ball a bit on the heel side of the face. I virtually never try to hit a full shot dead straight. I guess it stems from hearing for many years that the hardest shot to hit was one that was dead straight. Anyway, I seldom try to zero out the impact. I just do not see straight lines on full shots. But if that works for you, go with it.

I believe that top level players have long been familiar, at least intuitively, with these open-faced draws and shut-faced cuts. I recall Byron Nelson mentioning something about an open face when hitting a draw. We've all seen the slicer who keeps closing the face and slicing it even worse. Now at least he can know why.

You might say that the idea for a new simpler trackman swing was to try to do what Nicklaus might have tried to do if he had somehow known about the trackman principles. Remember, Nicklaus said he lined up his body where he wanted the ball to start (a logical way to try to dial in swing path) and aim the face where he wanted the ball to finish. That is a reasonable way to dial in face since returning the face at impact to its address position is something our subconscious mind might find easy to register (e.g., like hitting a pool ball). If Nicklaus had known the trackman laws, would he have adjusted his shot-shaping rules accordingly? Who knows? Maybe yes. Would he now aim the face, not at the target line, but half way between the path and the target? Maybe yes. It would be logical. It would be logical and consistent with trackman.

Before I tested this "Nicklaus with trackman" theory, I had a couple of more little problems to adjust and think about. Actually, they were not that small. Given the precision required, they are, in my opinion, two of the most significant. The first is the really devilish difficulty of aiming a golf club — any of them. You have thirteen clubs and they are all set up differently. They have different lofts, different lies, different shapes, different offsets, different degrees that the shaft leans in front of the face (or maybe even behind). They may even "help" you by opening or closing the face or "off-setting the face" (just my opinion, but the manufacturers are really "messing with our minds" when they do this). Compound this by the problem of the side-on alignment with a circular swing path. Clearly, golf has severe aiming problems. It explained to me why every golfer I have even mentioned it to has admitted that they have at some time stood over a shot and looked down at the face and thought "something's wrong – that just doesn't look right." I wonder how our subconscious minds deal with those kinds of doubts?

What would be the best way to deal with the aiming issue? The best, and only way I knew, was by use of two of the world's simplest training aids. The first is called a club face aimer. They're used in club repair and club making. It's a magnet you can attach to the sweet spot of your own club. A stick, maybe eight inches long, comes out of the center of the magnet and shows you exactly where the club face is aligned. You should get one and play around with it on each of your clubs separately - because all of them are a little different. Get used to how each of them look when you get them lined up on the exact line you want. Notice how it feels in your grip when the face is lined up perfectly. Burn those images and sensations into your mind. It is ridiculously important. There may be no fundamentals in golf, but if there were one, it would be ( in my opinion) club face alignment at address.

There was another question I needed to think about – aligned to what? Obviously not the target line any more, but the target line was still very, very important. For me, it was the spot on the ball that I wanted the sweet spot to contact. I decided that it should be on the equator of the ball and then just slightly to the inside for draws or slightly to the outside for fades. I try to relate it to my trackman ideas. For example, if I am going to try to hit that baby two degrees/one degree draw, I imagine that sweet spot to hit one-half of a dimple to the inside of the ball on the equator. For the four degrees/two degrees draw, I try to move the impact point another half a dimple inside. Of course, it is just the opposite of these for fades. Do I know that there is any real scientific validity to these numbers? No, of course I do not. Do I even know that the equator of the golf ball should be the initial point of contact of the face? No. But it made sense to me and that may well be the most important thing.

There is a second training aid that I believe you will find indispensable in getting your club face alignment at address perfect for you personally  every time - the ordinary alignment stick, but I use them in a  much different than I see others using them.  Try placing the stick on the target side of the ball directly pointing at your ultimate target (not necessarily your starting line unless you are attempting to "zero everything out").  I believe that sometimes we over-complicate golf by not recognizing that at its essence it is simply an aiming game and it is the aiming of the club face itself that is predominantly at issue and not the shoulders, hips, feet, or other body sections.  I don't know who came up with the  "railroad tracks" or parallel left ideas on alignment but I believe they are overly-simplistic.  I believe these ideas are taught to beginners because they are superficially logical. I suggest at least experimenting with alignments of hips, shoulders and feet that your body, guided by your subconscious mind would naturally step into in anticipation of making  sideways athletic throwing motions to a target ( i.e., skipping a stone across a pond, underhand softball fast pitch, sidearm basketball pass, infielder sidearm throw,  lead hand flinging a frisbee,  and others that that have been repeated over the last five hundred years of golf instruction).  Ask yourself this:  if you wanted to accomplish any of these athletic throws with as much power and precision as you could muster would you set yourself up with a railroad tracks alignment?  Possibly, but I doubt you'd try to be very exact about it.  Finally, consider this.  There is no mention of this railroad tracks alignment in <u>Five Lessons</u>.  It is so obvious I think we can be sure that Hogan considered it.  Before you get enamored with using those alignment sticks to aim your feet, shoulders, knees, hips, heels, or other body parts please look at video of Hogan, Trevino,  and Moe Norman at address (and impact) from down the line and ask yourself whether "railroad tracks" alignment is the best option for you.  I know it is a workable option, but for me and I think many others it is not the most athletic or even logical.

It is funny, but the first time I took these new ideas about club face alignment at address and impact with me to the range, I knew they would work. Not thought, or hoped, but was sure, absolutely sure, that they would work. And they did. And they continue to work for me to this day. Obviously, I still miss shots. The majority of the time for the same two reasons – most often, I just missed the sweet spot. We know from trackman that when we miss the sweet spot significantly that two-to-one ratio between path and face can go right out the window. But I can feel these and I know I don't have to reinvent my golf swing every time I mishit a shot. Here is a really important thing we should always remember – you will almost never hit a really bad shot if the ball is hit right out of the sweet spot. Your path and face angles have to be pretty messed up to do that. And that is the second major miss that I still have - I get really sloppy in target line and starting line visualization and club face alignment at address. There is no swing thought in the world that will fix that sloppiness.

There was one other little issue that I had to account for: I would have to actually aim the face just another shade to the right to account for the "how the ball comes off the face" phenomenon mentioned in the next chapter. And that bias shades to the right for righthanders, both with fades and draws. I think if you will think about it for a second it will make sense (come back to this after reading the next chapter).

I was ready. When I took it to the range, it worked the first shot, second shot, all the clubs, all the way through the bag. The process to follow on each shot was obvious. At first I would not worry about trajectory (that's a factor that can't be ignored because like most I use ball position to influence trajectory and ball position also effects club face and path at impact). But, to illustrate, I will summarize the thought process and visualization process for a 170 yard shot (carry). For me that is the top end of my seven-iron (or at least the club that in my set that has seven marked on it – when I was a kid it would have been marked five) So I pick the target and visualize the flight of the ball (let's say for me a baby draw). The baby draw is going to need to have two degrees in-to-out path. In my mind I align my body two degrees closed. Then I visualize the club coming into the ball – so I am visualizing that line that comes out of the sweet spot of the face, through the ball and on down the starting line. I pick the spot on the ball where that sweet spot will contact. Remember, for me with my baby draw – one-half dimple inside of the equator. I have just one swing thought for impact. Just connect the dots. That is what I call it. If the shot comes out as visualized, I just try to burn another one into my subconscious. If it does not, I try to note why. My first question always is sweet spot contact. Again, like most of us, I think, our biggest my biggest misses are sweet spot problems. I try to envision where on the face it hit: low, high, toe or heel. I blame it on my subconscious and remind myself to do more skill drills to improve sweet spot contact (I will talk about those in a later chapter). The other misses are generally the sloppy aiming ones (normally starting line). These rarely occur in practice when I can set down an alignment stick between the ball and target and can have such a clear reference point for aligning the club face at address. [If you follow this discussion and the following chapter it will be obvious that I rarely align that leading edge with that actual target line - that line is pointing to where I want the ball to finish, not start]. Since I started the system, I have yet to get to the point where I thought that a miss might have been caused by a technique issue (I do not call aiming the face technique; I just call it aiming now). Accordingly, I have not had to think about technique in a year-and-a-half. In any case, I think it more than ironic that I spent more than fifty years searching for techniques that would eliminate my golf problems. Yet I came to hit the ball far better than I ever have in my life my ignoring any thought of technique. Thankfully, for me the search is finally over.

# CHAPTER 3

## CLUB FACE ALIGNMENT AT ADDRESS – THE MIND-BLOWING TRUTH THAT IS VIRTUALLY NEVER TALKED ABOUT AND NEVER TAUGHT: COMBINED WITH KNOWLEDGE OF THE BALL FLIGHT LAWS IT CAN REVOLUTIONIZE YOUR BALL-STRIKING

This chapter and the previous one are the most important in this book. Skip the rest if you like. But (in my opinion) whether you are a beginner or a tour player, these two chapters can change the way that you look at the golf swing and remarkably improve your ball-striking. Seriously. Understanding it fully takes a little bit of imagination and mental work but I believe you will find it well worth the effort for the rest of your golfing life.

The starting point for this inquiry is what has been taught about club face alignment at address for, I would claim, the past five hundred years. It is the same thing that is taught today. At address the beginner is told to line the club face up perpendicular to the target line – specifically the leading edge of an iron is to be set up perpendicular to the target line. And this makes sense – think of how one would logically visualize striking a pool ball in a straight line, without any side spin or over spin with a cue tip. You would reasonably and logically set the face of that cue tip perpendicular to the target line directly behind the center of the ball at its equator. You can then move that perpendicular striking face straight back and through the target line. This is the most efficient and logical way to do it. I cannot think of any other logical way to go about it. Anyway, it was the way I was taught and the way virtually all golfers have been taught throughout the the ages.

Early on I assumed that striking a golf ball was subject to logical rules. I believed that I logically should be able to set that club face up perpendicular to the target line, with a neutral grip, line my hips, feet and shoulders up square (i.e., "railroad tracks" body alignment) and wouldn't it be easy to strike the ball straight down the line, just like with the pool ball? Wrong, and very wrong. When I tried it the ball started left. Sometimes it would go straight left, sometimes it left then curved right. I know now that in both cases the club face was pointing left at the point that mattered – we know now from science that it is the instant the ball leaves the club face that matters. Whether it stayed left or curved right depended on the relationship between that club face angle and the club path (assuming sweet spot contact). But neither I, nor those who were helping me, understood what was causing the ball to start left. Unfortunately we attributed it to "technique" faults. The one most commonly raised was "over the top." We didn't know — we didn't have launch monitors or video cameras. All we knew was to set up with the leading edge of the club face perpendicular to the target line. [note: Again, one thing that should be mentioned at this point. All of this assumes sweet-spot contact. If the ball significantly misses the sweet spot then other complicating factors such gear effect come into play].

I now know now exactly why that ball started left. Here is the easiest way I know to explain it. When I laid that club face down perpendicular to the target line, I was setting up failure. Try this experiment. Set the club face behind the ball comfortably but perpendicular to an exact extension of the the target line. When I do so comfortably with my own seven-iron its leading edge sits almost exactly one inch behind the center of the core of the golf ball if you dropped that center straight down to the ground on the target line. Even more importantly the sweet spot of that seven-iron is now almost exactly one and a half inches from the center of the core of the golf ball. Now visualize how the club face moves from that address position through impact. It closes – the toe passes the heel – it doesn't do so because of the player trying to rotate the forearms (I suppose you can speed up that process conscious forearm rolling but it all happens so fast that nobody knows how much, if any, face closure you can consciously add). It closes because of the way the club is designed and the nature of the instrument (a heavier weight on the side of a light stick being swung in a circle). We will have to trust the scientists on that. In addition, by the time the ball is fully compressed and actually leaves at the moment of truth it has closed even more. So how much face closure are we dealing with here? I don't know - I seriously doubt that anybody really knows and no doubt it varies with every golfer (maybe if a player was strong enough he could "hold off" some or all of that natural rotation of the face - but why would he or she want to?). I am just speculating based primarily on my own experience but I believe that for the average player who makes no attempt to hold off the natural closing of the face we are talking about a couple of degrees. Not important? You tell me. With the absolute precision required in a full golf shot a couple of degrees is profoundly important.

When I first heard about this idea of face alignment and how the ball left the club face, I was shocked. Why had nobody explained it to me? Wouldn't this be a tremendously important consideration in a game requiring the unbelievable precision of golf? Wouldn't it be more important than say whether your left foot was flared exactly at twenty-two degrees? Wouldn't it be something that should be demonstrated to and explained and burned into the subconscious mind of every golfer?

The second part of the puzzle was equally fascinating. I was watching a video made by Mike Bennett and Andy Plummer (the

Stack and Tilt guys) and listening to a section where they talk about there being no fundamentals in golf (other than, they say, the ball flight laws). They mentioned that many great ball-strikers set the club face behind the ball in significantly different directions. To my mind the differences were extraordinary. They mention that relative to the target line Steve Elkington sets the club face up more than thirty degrees open and K.J. Choi sets the club face up two degrees closed. I have no idea how they made these measurements. I do know it is very difficult for an observer to see exactly where a player's club face is pointing at address. It's often even difficult for the player himself to tell.

In any event, it got me looking at all kinds of golf swings and how the face was set at address. Again, it's really hard to tell if you are not the player and difficult even if you are. Unfortunately no one measured these things over the years (except maybe Bennet and Plummer). And I think that is scary because I now realize how ridiculously important it is. I believe most good players set the face down a little bit open. I think that over the years they have learned to do this subconsciously. I think a few have done it consciously. Maybe they experimented with setting the face down a little open and noticed how much easier it made it to keep the ball from starting left. Maybe they realized that it was open to the target line but, they would not worry about why, at least as long as got the results they wanted. I looked at my address and realized that I tended to line up the face just a little closed, like K.J. Choi. I imagine that there are some good ball-strikers who consistently line the club face up exactly the way it has always been taught with the leading edge exactly perpendicular to the target line. I believe that included in that group would be players who like to practice with lots of alignment aids to assist them with a visual reference as they attempt to set that leading edge exactly perpendicular to the target line.

To me the most amazing thing about learning about these differences in club face alignment at address was what it implicitly meant. It meant that the ability of the subconscious mind to calibrate how to get the strike to conform to the ball flight laws was simply extraordinary. The minute variances in variables like grip, stance, weight shift, ball position, etc. (the "standard fundamentals") that had to be adjusted by the subconscious was simply staggering. That the golf swings of two different world class players who set the club face behind the ball aimed in two wildly divergent directions would look identical was, I thought, remote, and of course they don't.

I can't say which of the club face address alignment positions (open, closed or square) is superior. No one can answer that question - they are all "workable" options. But I can say that I remembered over the years hearing about a player who liked to set the face down open. I had heard about accounts from other players who noticed that he did it and of just a few conversations, where he said he liked to do it. Who was it? You guessed it, Ben Hogan, although there is no mention of club face alignment at address in Five Lessons. I will throw this idea out for consideration. I have no idea but might club face alignment at address be called a "secret?" The reader may recall the quote, "it's there, if you know where to look."

So, with my new found knowledge about club face alignment at address, I went to the range and starting experimenting. I tried everything from closed to open to square, with all types of variations in between. I even tried variations that were so closed or open that I felt like the leading edge was almost parallel to the target line. For me personally I noticed that a closed or even "traditionally" square leading edge at address made it very easy to hit the shots I had always tried to fight off with "better technique" - the pulls and "weaker" fades ( in the old days the start line of the ball was almost always left what I intended). But simply opening the face at address did for me what no other "technique" had ever even come close to. It immediately opened up for me the shot I most desired to repeat, the slight draw that starts to the right and comes back to the target.

I know it is something I should have figured out thirty years before. But I did not. I assumed that what the "experts" said was correct ( "you came a little over-the-top"). Nobody taught that and I was not smart enough to realize that with something so basic I could figure it out as well as anybody else could, even the gurus of golf. I ultimately came to the conclusion that a slightly open club face works best for me. It allows me to start the ball on the right line the most often. I will probably experiment some more with the Elkington very open address face more (with the face that open I never, ever hit the shot that has hurt me the most in the past – the out of control left-to-left darter. It might be worth occasionally losing one to the right to eliminate that feared double-bogey creator).

If you are going to begin to create your own new golf swing I believe you should begin with club face alignment at address. Open, closed, square? Experiment. Find out what works for you. Specifically find out what helps you get the ball started on the line you pick the most often. I strongly suggest slightly open. I have one caveat. I believe that there may be club face alignments that are so radical that they make achieving workable ball flight patterns either extremely difficult or even physically impossible. I am talking about the face being very closed. You may have seen this pattern. The new player has the common new player problem of severe out-to-in path and face open or even slightly closed (he or she may even have a true "over-the-top" issue). The ball starts left and curves right so, to get rid of the slice, he does the "logical" thing to stop the ball from curving right – he closes the face. It may curve even more. He closes it some more. I am not an expert on the new ball flight laws, but I know enough about them to make good use of them for myself. I know enough to realize that if you set the club face more than thirty degrees closed to the target line at address, there is no conceivable way you can create the impact conditions that I consider necessary to produce a perfect baby draw – a swing path two degrees in-to-out and a club face one degree open to the target line. I doubt that it is physically possible to get your hands that far ahead of the club face at impact and certainly not with any workable launch angles.

To summarize this chapter, if you decide to redesign your own golf swing with your own personal fundamentals, I strongly suggest you begin by examining your club face alignment at address and consider the ramifications of it. Then combine it with the information about the ball flight laws from preceding chapter.

# CHAPTER 4

## YOUR GOLF SWING EVOLVES EVERY DAY OF YOUR LIFE

What is your golf swing? In my opinion, nothing more than the pattern of body movements that you use to perform your golf shots. Not just the arms, hands, legs or shoulders, but all parts of the body working together. While your conscious mind can influence those movements during any one shot, it is controlled primarily by your subconscious mind. How our subconscious minds work is not fully understood, or even well understood. Like virtually everything in life, the subconscious mind is not within the realm of human understanding - it's simply too complex. Think of the factors that might affect a golf swing at any one point in time - a group of body motions requiring incredible, even miraculous, precision. How about every golf shot you have ever hit, every golf shot you have ever seen hit, every swing thought you have ever had, how you learned basic movement skills such as walking and standing around bouncing the ball off the face of your wedge when you were twelve-years-old (or not doing that), your age, innate hand-eye coordination, strength, flexibility, what you had for breakfast, the results of previous shot, your playing partner's rattling change in his pocket, the temperature, or an argument you had with your spouse. The number of factors is not just large – it is virtually infinite.

When I think about this inherent complexity, it convinces me of a number of truths about the golf swing that, if you can come to grips with them, can increase your knowledge about how the subconscious mind and therefore your golf swing works. And if you can do that, maybe you can use your conscious mind to influence your subconscious mind's ability to create the golf shots you want. Initially, I am sure that every golf swing you make throughout your life will be different. You will never pass the same point twice. You will never have the same amount of strength, flexibility and hand-eye coordination (or the myriad of other factors that play a part) two days in a row or two shots in a row. Your golf swing will evolve continuously in response to these changes. Do you ever wonder why swing thoughts which work one day stop working the next? Or why a swing thought that never worked before suddenly becomes magical? No one knows the answer to these questions, but I think it may have something to do with this evolution of our golf swings (which is really, in my opinion, nothing more than the evolution of our subconscious minds).

The other day I was on the practice chipping green and I thought about something we used to do all the time when I was a teenager. We used to stand around bouncing a ball off the face of our wedges. I don't know why we did it. I know we did it a lot. Some kids could do it off the face of their drivers. I think they learned it from watching Chi-Chi Rodriguez. You have seen Tiger Woods do it in commercials – he was really skilled at it. As far as I know kids have always done it when they learn golf. I see them doing it today. As far as I know, they don't really think about it or practice it in the way you would work on their regular golf swing. They just do it. I believe that wedge bouncing is a good demonstration of basic, instinctive hand-eye coordination. Nobody can teach it to you – you have either have it or you don't, but you can improve it. Every twelve-year-old boy I have ever played with had it to a pretty high degree. I think my own ability for wedge bouncing was pretty average when I was a teenager. I could get twenty-five bounces in a row without much trouble, stop the ball on the wedge, spin it a little, vary the height of the ball, but not much more. I quit doing it for almost fifty years.

Anyway, the other day, I thought back on my teenage wedge bouncing (I was alone on the chipping green) and reached the face of my wedge under a ball. First attempt - second bounce misses the sweet spot by an inch and the ball careens off left. Second attempt – third bounce misses sweet spot by an inch and ball careens of to the right. I gave it up after about five tries. I just couldn't do it anymore.

I was embarrassed (even though no one was around) and more than a little sad because I think I know what it means. It means that my basic instinctive hand-eye coordination skill has diminished, severely diminished, since I was twelve. Now, I am sixty-four and it will not be coming back. I have lost forever a very large amount of an essential inborn skill for quality ball-striking – basic hand-eye coordination. I believe that gradual diminishment of that skill occurs in everybody. It's not just a loss of strength or club head speed that keeps players over fifty from being normally competitive on the PGA or LPGA tours. It's the diminishment of a whole host of essential skills including hand-eye coordination, strength, flexibility, endurance and concentration. My golf swing, body and mind at sixty-four are so different from what they were at twelve I could almost be said to be a different person.

Recognizing that my golf swing was in a constant state of evolution (at my age it might be better expressed as a state of deterioration) has allowed me to find some truths that have helped my own golf swing. First, I know, at least to my own satisfaction, why I need to keep reviewing swing thoughts (from many, many sources) to find workable solutions for my present swing. Second, I know why really good ball strikers (such as Hogan and Moe Norman) normally kept notebooks of their swing thoughts. Third, I know why sometimes, like every other player that ever lived, I hit the shot for which I have absolutely no explanation – the horrible mishit that comes seemingly out of nowhere. During most of my life these shots could have led to major swing rebuilds. A more productive response would probably be "you know, I think my foot slipped." Sound familiar? Now I just recognize that its cause may just be beyond human understanding. Now I just try to find it and hit the next shot. Fourth, I know why in spite of hitting balls often daily for over fifty years, though it happens far less than it used to, when I hit the first couple of full shots of the day, I sometimes feel like I'm doing something doing completely alien to me – like I have never played golf before. At one time I assumed something was wrong with my swing. Now, I just keep hitting balls until I feel warmed up and comfortable. Then I can turn it over to my subconscious. Finally, I know why in my mind, I will never find the secret, a secret, a technique, or a technique barrier. I will never make a perfect swing or hit a prefect shot. I may get the ball in the hole but if that happens from more than ten feet, I will be reminded that the largest portion of that can be easily chalked up to luck and probability. I know that I will probably never feel completely comfortable with my golf swing, at least not for more than a week at most. I know I will have to dig that scoundrel out of the ground every day that I go to the practice range for as long as I live. But, I also know that I will always find what is best for my golf swing better than the combined efforts of all the golf instructors and swing schools on the planet. In fact, the actual knowledge that it takes (most of it trackman information and ball flight laws) is very, very limited. I am doing it for myself and believe that you can and should do it for yourself.

# CHAPTER 5

## GREAT BALL-STRIKERS ARE NORMALLY INNOVATIVE EXPERIMENTERS

If you look at Hogan's swing in Power Golf and then compare it to his swing in Five Lessons you might be shocked by the obvious distinctive differences. As a younger man he used a stronger grip; substantially stronger (left thumb on the right side of the shaft). To fight his hook he switched to a weaker grip (left thumb straight down the shaft) which he said was recommended to him by Henry Picard. In Power Golf his backswing was long and upright. By the time of Five Lessons it was much shorter and flatter. Part of this was no doubt due to the bus wreck (his golf swing was forced to evolve quickly if he was to keep playing). He had his characteristic wide stance in both Power Golf and Five Lessons, but if you look at videos from the forties, fifties and sixties you will often see a considerably narrower stance than that displayed in the books. He also moved the ball around in his stance considerably more than he described in Five Lessons. That much is evident from the existing videos and still pictures, although some of what is being displayed there is no doubt due to camera angles and the trajectory of the shots being displayed. He explained the "secret" of the cupped left wrist at the top to Life Magazine, but you can find video both before and after that time where the left wrist at least appears flat at the top. I don't intend to dispute anything that Hogan said about his own swing feelings, but I do think this does demonstrate that Hogan was a great experimenter. He wasn't afraid to consider ideas of others; I assume other pros whom he respected. But most of all, he was not afraid to try his own unconventional ideas (I am not aware of anyone recommending to students the cupped left wrist prior to Hogan).

As far as I know, Hogan's bent for experimentation remained in him for his entire life. From all accounts he was still digging and experimenting into his eighties. I seriously doubt that he ever thought, "You know, that material we came up with in Five Lessons was pretty good, maybe I should just stick with that." I have often thought that Five Lessons was misnamed. If anyone ever asks, here is the title I suggest: "Five Lessons: The Fundamentals of Hogan's Golf Swing as Relayed to a Ghost-writer in the Summer of 1955 (at least the ones he was willing to give up)." I am only half kidding - it would not surprise me at all if it were discovered that Hogan had never actually read Five Lessons.

Moe Norman was also apparently a great experimenter, especially in his younger, formative years. He was not afraid the try the hugely unconventional one-plane arm and shaft plane in spite of ridicule he must have taken from his peers. He also was not afraid to experiment with perhaps his most unusual move - "setting the club head about eight inches behind the ball and slightly inside the line." He allegedly said, "I don't know why — I just woke up one day and started doing it."

I think it is interesting and informative that both of them did huge amounts of experimentation with their equipment. Hogan put the reminder wires in his grips. Both liked to use very heavy clubs and bent their irons into unusually flat lie angles. Both of them found their own way and then did it their own way. As I've said once I got enough confidence to look for my own way and follow it, my own game has remarkably improved.

I suggest that you do the same. No one can show you the way – not Leadbetter, or Foley or the Moe Norman Golf School, definitely not me. Either they or I can only provide you with overall swing concepts or swing thoughts (hopefully never positions) that worked for them, or indirectly, for one of their students. I am not saying to ignore them. Put them in your arsenal of overall swing concepts and swing thoughts. Experiment with the swing thoughts (normally you can tell within a few balls). If they help, wear them out. Keep using them until you need something else. If they don't help, file them away. You will have a different swing and set of issues tomorrow. But never treat any swing concept or swing thought as gospel.

# CHAPTER 6

## A YEAR OF THE MOE NORMAN GOLF ACADEMY

In the early nineties I broke down and attended a Moe Norman Golf Academy. I can't tell you which incarnation of the Moe Norman or single plane school it was. All I remember is that we had the "single plane" set-up, a wide stance, and gripped the club in the palm of the right hand with big grips. I bought into the marketing and got a full set of clubs with the big grips, slightly longer shafts as I remember, and flat lies because we stood so far from the ball. The technique was very easy to learn and within three days at the school, I was comfortable with it. By then I was also comfortable enough to play golf with it in spite of feeling just a bit "goofy" with it.

The year that I played with it, I played okay – not great, just okay. I hit a lot of really straight iron shots – the misses were slight. And the same was true with the woods. Very consistent — very straight. The problem was that I didn't need straight. I needed the driver to carry 250, not the same old 235. But now with the new method my driver might carry 230 when I nutted it — maybe just 225. I was becoming a driving machine -- but it was a short driving machine. I went back to the Moe Norman school the next summer to work on the distance aspect.

At that time video cameras were just coming into vogue and on the first day of the school we all got videoed. It was the first time I had seen my golf swing on video and like most people who see their swings for the first time, I was shocked. I had roughly the same body type as Moe. What I saw in the camera, at least in the fuzzy screen, was an excellent impersonation of a sixty-five year Moe Norman. The problem was I was forty-five years old at the time. At sixty-five, Moe had a short, flat, three-quarter swing. The instructors at the school, at least the one I attended, weren't flexible with opinions or in suggesting workable options that might work for me, so soon after that school I got rid of the clubs and moved on to the next system.

I now know very clearly that there are many easy, workable options which could have helped with the distance issue and most are simply common sense. The first would have been to ditch the fat grips and put the grip back more into the fingers of my hands. That and lightening the grip pressure might have enhanced club head speed. Moe purportedly said he liked to hold the club "like drawing blood." Sure, while that might enhance club face control for some, might it be at the expense of club head speed? The biggest speed bump could likely have come from just making a fuller shoulder turn. Narrowing the wide stance could have also freed that shoulder turn up considerably also. I was certainly well capable of doing it. I have since seen pictures where Moe did make a full turn when he was younger. I think Moe shortened his swing as he aged not because he wanted to, but because he was losing flexibility. So, if I learned anything from my experience, it's that if you are going to "model" a golf swing, don't pick the sixty-five-year-old version of your model. And don't be afraid to use modifications to the model. Experiment! Use your common sense. I don't suggest modeling anyone, but if you feel like you have to do so use common sense.

Here's my favorite story about Moe Norman: A friend of mine once went an exhibition to watch him hit shots. It was being put on by one of the Natural Golf School promoters and most of the audience was potential students for the school. After watching Moe hit an endless stream of seemingly perfect shots for a half-hour, a man in the crowd asked, “Hey Moe, if someone was to come to the school and learn everything about your swing there and hit balls every day for say, two years, would they be able to hit the ball like you?” My friend said Moe smiled, looked away from the man, shook his head and said in that sing-song voice you hear on the videos, “Can’t be done, can’t be done.” I don’t believe Moe was conceited. I think he just knew.

# CHAPTER 7

## RULE NUMBER ONE FOR BUILDING YOUR OWN GOLF SWING – CHALLENGE EVERYTHING, ESPECIALLY THE PLATITUDES OF THE EXPERTS

I know you have heard this one, "All the great ones look exactly the same at impact." It sounds good – they sort of look the same. There is an implication when they say it that if we can just get you in that "pro" perfect impact position you will master the golf swing. The problem is that it is simply not true, particularly if you look at comparisons of players hitting their drivers. You might want to take a look at players like Michelle Wie, Rory Mclloy and Dustin Johnson at impact. You will notice significant differences in their hand positions and shaft lean. Good players learn to adjust their shaft lean to change their launch angles: more lean to launch it lower and less lean to launch it higher. Some "reverse" the lean to launch it really high (e.g., Jamie Sadlowski).

The same is true with irons. There is a former tour player who teaches his students that the best ball-strikers all have a "low point" in their swings that is approximately four inches in front of the ball. So he teaches his students to learn to move their divots forward so that their lowest points are similar (reflected by the lowest part of the divot). I think I understand why this training might be helpful to some students to improve their ball-striking. We all know what happens when the low point doesn't get up to the ball. We hit it fat — one of the most damaging shots in golf. We all do that at some times early in our training when our hand-eye coordination is not yet well-developed. I believe that most of us learn to move that low point forward to avoid the dreaded fat shot. I agree that often one of the best things we can do to help a novice improve his ball-striking almost immediately is to help him move the low point forward (with a little forward shaft lean) which avoids the fat shot while at the same time making sure to take a divot (which will normally avoid the thin shot). I believe this is a wonderful drill for untrained players. However, I strongly disagree that a four-inch forward swing bottom is a "perfect" impact position or a fundamental of golf. It simply isn't.

If you look back into the history of the great ball-strikers (unfortunately with most of the older players we are lacking really clear video of impact) you will find much less forward lean than in modern players. Do not take my word for it. Take a look at video of Bobby Jones, Sam Snead, Ben Hogan and Moe Norman. You also might remember how the old school players were often pickers. They preferred thinner divots or even in some cases no divots at all – just to "brush the grass" even with their irons. You might also want to think about modern LPGA players who normally have less forward shaft lean than their PGA counterparts. Why? I'm not sure, but one reason could be that with less club head speed they need the extra launch angle created by having the shaft more vertical and the low point further back at impact.

Another thing you might want to think about in setting up your own ideal impact conditions is this. Consider this example. In his best years they say Tiger Woods hit his driver with a little downward angle of attack, a couple of degrees. His club head speed was around one hundred twenty miles per hour. But he needed control with his driver, not extra launch angle. So he had significant forward shaft lean with his driver for control. But what about the player with ninety mile per hour swing speed with a great need for carry distance with his driver and to launch it higher? To maximize his driver carry length, he more needs to get rid of his forward shaft lean. To maximize his driver carry distance he will need the swing to bottom out behind the ball and catch the teed up ball on the upswing.

With respect to the lower swing speed player the same principle also applies to a lesser degree to his irons, although obviously he doesn't want the low point on an iron shot off the ground to be behind the ball. But with the four-inch forward low point the lower speed player may not generate enough club head speed with his irons to achieve his optimum launch. He or she is likely far better off to emulate the old school pickers or sweepers with less shaft lean. Does it make any sense at all to put these two very different players in identical "perfect" impact alignments?

# CHAPTER 8

## WHY YOU SHOULD ABANDON THE GOLFING MACHINE AND OTHER HARD "SCIENCE-BASED" GOLF SWING THEORIES

The first "scientist" that I knew of who tried to apply science to the golf swing was Mindy Blake. We looked at what that led to in a previous chapter. The second "scientist" who I became aware of who tried to apply scientific principles to golf was Homer Kelley in The Golfing Machine. He believed the human body could to be trained to perform like a golfing machine. He didn't describe the machine, but described 24 component systems that could be blended together to produce a certain number of workable options. I can't remember how many options but it was something like 64, or 82, or 88. Surely anyone intelligent enough to unearth all this information could explain why my shots almost always started left of my intended target line and it could be easily fixed.

So, I found a copy of The Golfing Machine and set out in search of the answer. The problem is that to someone who is not technically minded, the book is incomprehensible. It's not just me - I have heard this from dozens of people. Certain things he said made sense – a flat left wrist at impact was essential in all his systems (I now believe that it is something very common and can be used by virtually anybody, but I no longer believe it is essential). He talked about lag being indispensable (I now believe that it is an observable phenomenon, but not an essential) (see e.g., Tom Watson's golf swing – at least with regard to holding late lag).

I couldn't understand Mr. Kelley's book so in about 1974 I went to one of his devotees, a certified teacher of The Golfing Machine, a GMSE or whatever he was called. He couldn't clear up anything for me. I remember him drawing a little stick man for me — a little guy striking a ball with a little club. I guess he was "the golfing machine." We did agree that someone could apply a two-lever system (I will admit that the lever principle is the only mechanical principle I remotely understand) to employ extra power into a golf ball. I tried to feel that lever system work as I hit balls and while it made logical sense to me, it didn't improve or diminish my ball-striking.

Over the years I gathered more of The Golfing Machine information from various sources. It appears that Mr. Kelley's ideas still have quite a few followers, or, as I call them, interpreters. They managed to teach me about power accumulators (I could understand that parts of the human body could "accumulate" energy which could then be potentially released at the right time). I remember the "pressure points" – they called them P1, P2, P3 and P4 rather than just the first knuckle of right forefinger or the left arm pit. I tried to use the four pressure points they identified to produce the extra five miles per hour of club head speed that I thought I needed. I could feel the pressure in the pressure points, feel it retained, then feel it released. In the "biggie", as I remember P3 was (the index finger of the right hand), I thought I could feel it retained right into impact. But nothing happened – I didn't hit it any better or any worse for that matter. His seemed like good ideas, just not helpful good ideas.

One place where I did adopt some of The Golfing Machine ideas was, oddly enough, in the short game. One of the things Kelley's devotees start their teaching with is what they call a basic motion. It is just a little chip with a little forward shaft lean and flat left wrist. They teach it as something you can use for your basic chip motion and since it was consistent with standard chipping technique taught generally at the time (ball back, weight forward, flat left wrist, forward leaning shaft). [I now believe that that standard chipping instruction, drilled into millions of unfortunate victims, may be some of the worst instruction given in the history of golf]. I employed this standard chipping methodology for many years. It makes sense, doesn't it? The chip swing is just a mini version of the big swing? It worked okay. I hit a lot of serviceable, even great chips. It works fine as long as you had a great lie. The problem is it doesn't work so well when the lie is really sketchy. What do you do when the lie is downhill, the grain in long and right back into you? When the ball is on hardpan with very little grass, if any?

The course where I played most often at the time had a lot of really thin areas around the greens. Sometimes the ground would be wet, sometimes even muddy. I might face a shot requiring 15 feet of carry, 15 feet of run to think about and a muddy thin lie. If you employ the standard chipping technique as I did or The Golfing Machine basic motion to that shot, you were a dead man. An all too likely result was sticking the blade in the ground behind the ball. You might get a perfect impact occasionally. You also might blade it occasionally, options that I couldn't live with.

When I chunked those little shots, my original reaction was to think, something was wrong with the way I was employing the technique. So I experimented with ball position, how much weight to set left, whether to open the stance or open the blade. Still the results were always too inconsistent. But never did I think might be an inherent flaw in the technique or that Mr. Kelley's basic motion might be a particularly dangerous technique to apply to that particular shot. Recently I began to think about using Mr. Kelley's basic motion as a chipping technique and I can only conclude now it was horrible idea. No, the chip shot is not just a miniature version of the full swing. Chipping and pitching are way, way more creative than that.

Beside the chipping green when I now practice, is a low area where the water runs off. Some parts of it have a little grass growing. Some parts have no grass. After a good rain it is just a little mud hole. Then no one ever goes near it. That is except me. Since I have been using my new method of chipping and pitching without "fundamentals" (I will explain it in a later chapter on short shots), I use it to check how far I have come in the short game area. I use my imagination to come up with a way to hit it cleanly. Most times I think I stand the shaft up on the toe of the wedge and visualize that mini-sweet spot out on the toe, contacting an unblocked point on the ball. It is still a brutally hard shot, but, I am guessing, I can get up and down seventy-five percent of the time out of that "mud-hole." The more I work at, the better my subconscious will get at it and getting a playable result out of the infinite variety of other little short shots that exist.

Another thing that I have realized about the "scientists" golf theorists is, as far as I know, they are generally not good ball-strikers themselves. They are often people who spend their lives in a left-brained career such as physics or math or engineering and then retire to work on a new project – solving the mystery of the golf swing. They begin with the left-brained assumption that (1) it is a "solvable" problem; and (2) that physics can solve it. I can't prove it, no one can, but I remain convinced that it is not a solvable problem – it would be a problem well beyond human comprehension. And if it was comprehensible, the solution would not lie primarily in the laws of physics, but in those incredible, God-like human computers, the most amazing things in the universe, our subconscious minds.

I never met Mr. Kelley. I am sure as a very nice man. But if I should happen to meet him in heaven I have a question for him. Have you ever been practicing or playing and hitting a ball off a tee – usually a driver – when this happens? You are at the top of your backswing or just starting down when the ball falls off the tee. It's too late to stop your downswing. I've had it happen to me, I don't know, four or five times in fifty years, maybe more. I've seen it happen to other good players, maybe four or five other times, and what happens? In each case, the player at least hits it somewhat solid. I've never seen anyone whiff it. Sometimes the player gets a playable shot out of it. And it's not that I was trapped into the swing I started down with – I could feel the body lurch as my subconscious mind tried to get the club head on that moving ball. Or those trick shot artists that can throw a ball up and hit a playable drive down the fairway with a driver? Which one of those 88 workable options were being used to strike those moving golf balls? What part of it is "technique" and what part the inconceivably brilliant hand-eye coordination that we all have to a large degree?

While I was working on this chapter a golfer with a strong bent for science came to my mind. He won two tour events although he was, by all accounts, not a good putter. He was considered a ball-striking genius by his peers. He was a devotee of Homer Kelley and The Golfing Machine. He was the interesting but eccentric Mac O'Grady. Obviously, someone who was considered a ball-striking genius learned something valuable from The Golfing Machine. So I googled Mac O'Grady and found a video from the late eighties of Gary McCord explaining what Mac O'Grady was up to. He was working on a project called MORAD – a further and deeper explanation into and explanation of the principles of Homer Kelley. Mr. McCord said in the video the O'Grady was working with a number of tour players and that MORAD, when it was finally released, would revolutionize golf instruction. I thought about Blake's "technique barriers" idea. Was the key finally here? I recently heard that MORAD still hasn't been released and I'm not sure what happened to the tour players he was working with. I guess they're still clearing up a few points – like maybe exactly how that trick shot artist hits that moving ball.

I'll mention one final thought about Mac O'Grady. I remember when he played the tour there were a lot of stories about his physical skills. He could break par both left-handed and right-handed. I am not overly confident about many things, but one thing I am pretty sure of is that anyone who can accomplish that outrageous feat has a highly unusual degree of innate hand-eye coordination. You may be aware that an inordinately high number of great ball-strikers have or had very high degrees of ambidexterity (e.g., Hogan). I can only speculate here, but is it possible that Mac O'Grady could have been an even better ball-striker if he had never heard of Mr. Kelley? One final question about Mac O'Grady: How do we explain such great innate hand-eye coordination but such poor (relative) putting. Could an obsession with technique in putting have cancelled out his touch ( maybe the ultimate display of hand-eye coordination)?

So when I look for ideas that might help me, I don't look to the golf "scientists" anymore - I believe that they are inevitably classic cases of "too much information" and are conceptually too complex. The most workable ideas for me come from the simplest conceptually and the more right-brained thinkers: actual pure ball-strikers like "Wild" Bill Mehlhorn, Sam Snead, and believe it or not, even the inimitable Count Yogi.

# CHAPTER 9

## HOW THE WORST GOLF LESSON I EVER HAD TURNED OUT TO HELP THE MOST

An instruction book was published about twenty years ago that greatly fascinated me. I will not mention the title or the author because I don't want to embarrass him. I don't know that what I am about to say would embarrass him, but I am not going to take any chances.

The author was what I think even he would admit, a Hogan zealot. He was one of those people who could only refer to him as Mr. Hogan. His book explained his theory that Mr. Hogan's secret was in his pivot – the exact and very precise way that he pivoted into his backswing and transitioned into his downswing. The book was well-written, well-thought out and precisely detailed. The author was a well-respected teacher and extremely analytical. Prior to moving on to his studies of Mr. Hogan's swing, he had been a Golfing Machine teacher. So I did the only logical thing I could do. I arranged to meet with him and drove 400 miles across two states to his teaching facility.

First, we played nine holes. It was evident he was an excellent ball-striker and he still played professionally. He was the reigning State Open Champion of the state we were in. After we played we went back to his practice facility for a lesson. His practice facility might have been the best I've ever seen. It was secluded at the end of a long driving range. You could hit balls off of turf or go inside a barn-like structure and hit balls out of a hitting bay. A "barn door" could be slid open, the balls actually hit out into the back of the range and the ball flight observed. The best part was that he had cameras installed at all of the angles he considered important: caddy view, down the line, from directly behind the player and from directly above the player. There were all hooked up to a monitor where he could check the angles and positions any time he wanted. It was obvious that he spent a lot of time working on his own "Mr. Hogan pivot" here and he obviously had good results. I was impressed.

So we set to work. He got out a copy of Five Lessons and showed me in the picture on page 41 of how the feet were to be set apart the width of the shoulders when the golfer prepared to play a standard five-iron shot. Absolute precision would be helpful, wouldn't it? He got out a yardstick and we measured my "perfect" five-iron width and actually marked it on the stick. He actually held the stick up against my shoulders. Then we turned to the ball position diagram on page 125 and marked the correct ball position for the standard five-iron shot. He made an appropriate mark on the stick of where my ball position would be in my new five-iron stance.

We took my five-iron, went outside and I tried to get used to the new sensations. For me it was very, very odd. When we laid the yardstick down my new stance was super-wide; wider than it had ever been even with my driver. But even stranger to me was how far forward in the stance the ball was. I protested, but he assured me that it felt so odd just because of how far off I had been before.

We worked on the pivot for a few minutes. I had worked on it when I got the book so I thought I understood it pretty well. So I set up to hit the first ball. Guess what? Cold top. Second ball? Same thing. For thirty minutes I couldn't get the ball in the air. I think I finally managed to hit a very weak cut by sliding my head forward about a foot and a half on the downswing. My time was up by them. He gave me my yardstick to use when I practiced. He assured me that it would get better as my pivot improved. It goes without saying that the trip home was quite depressing. I used my yardstick and new pivot for about a week until I was completely convinced that it would never work. I moved back to whatever I was using before I'd read his book. I didn't learn much at the time except, perhaps, I definitely wasn't Mr. Hogan.

Lately, though, I've realized that I learned a lot from this seemingly unfortunate experience. I now know that what we were doing with that yardstick and what that instructor was doing with all his camera angles, was just an elaborate form of "modeling" or positions instruction. We see a player who is a great ball-striker. We don't really understand what he is doing but if we copy identically his every position and move, we will hit it good also. It might work.

In my opinion it is one of the most dangerous forms of golf instruction. But why would it be a workable solution for the author of the Hogan pivot book and not me? Obviously he got something out of all those camera positions and angles, or, at least they didn't appear hurt him. Again, it is just my opinion, but I think he got lucky. Although he was a larger man than Mr. Hogan I think there was a proportionality there that allowed it to be a workable option for him too. With me, I am about the same height of Mr. Hogan but that's where any similarity ends. My shoulders are significantly broader. His arms are significantly longer. I am significantly thicker and he significantly more flexible. When I put this together and used common sense, I realized the ball would be relatively much more forward in the stance for me than Hogan and I would have had a dramatically greater challenge to get back to the ball at impact. By setting myself up like Hogan set himself up to succeed I was setting myself up to fail: it was really that simple. Would this have all changed if we had just moved the ball back a little and narrowed the stance? Maybe, but then, of course, we wouldn't have been modeling

Mr. Hogan. Could I have borrowed some, but not all of the ideas of that golf instructor who preached the "Hogan pivot" and intelligently applied it to my own golf swing (which I am clearly the best expert on)? Absolutely, and that is exactly what I should have done. What this golf lesson taught me was to not blindly mimic anyone, even great ball-strikers. Take ideas from them, but only the things that work for you. Beware of positions based instructions or trying to model anyone.

# CHAPTER 10

## IT CAME TIME FOR ME TO PUT THE LAG BABY TO BED — IT MIGHT BE TIME FOR YOU TO DO THE SAME

As far as I know, the concept of "lag" in the teaching of the golf swing didn't appear much, if at all, prior to 1960. Hogan didn't mention it in Five Lessons. We probably should learn something from the fact that he didn't mention it. I first became aware of it as a concept (although it wasn't called lag) in about 1968 when I came across a book by Joe Dante – Four Magic Moves to Winning Golf. What struck me at the time were stop actions pictures in the book of two players, each as they neared impact. Both were taken from face-on at the point in their downswings where their hands were passing their right thighs. In the first picture, that of a tour professional, there is still a marked angle between the left arm and the shaft. The lower body of the pro is much more active – his right heel is off the ground and his hips have opened. The player in the second picture looks quite different – the angle has released entirely and his lower body is inert. He is flat-footed and his hips face the ball. There were a couple of things expressed and implied by the text. As I took it, that phenomenon, the late retention of the left arm shaft angle, was the result of a scientific principle. It was given a name – something like conservation of angular momentum. It sounded impressive and powerful. What I drew from it was that by holding that angle until as late as possible the pro was able to release more energy; i.e., club head speed, into the ball. And that science could explain this power increase. How much of an increase were we talking about? I am still waiting for the answer to that question. It also appeared to suggest that the phenomenon of holding the angle could be enhanced through a more active lower body. I am still waiting on the proof of that. But one thing that I have consistently found to hold true is that if the player leaves his arms completely soft from the top (and I mean completely soft) and will just make an aggressive slinging motion with his body toward the target (think skipping a stone right-handed or throwing a frisbee left-handed) any lag issue will take care of itself.

The first I knew of this phenomenon being called lag is in The Golfing Machine where it is described this way: "It is simple, elusive, indispensable, without substitute or compensation and always present." I wrote a short e-book a couple of years ago titled Lag and the Economical Golf Swing. The book is nothing more than a simple model for an economical golf swing; i.e., one with a minimum of moving parts, with an impact position that mimics address and relies on the phenomenon of lag as the primary power source. I still think it's a workable model, one of an infinite variety of workable models (yes, I believe that number is infinite).

In the past two years I've changed my mind about lag, mainly because of my own experience in trying to "improve" my own and the extensive use of a video camera and a swing speed radar device. It may help you formulate your own ideas about this mysterious subject if I tell you what I've learned about it for myself. It might possibly save you a lot of wasted time. First, I think when we are talking about lag we are talking about club head speed at impact. I think it is irrelevant for any purpose other than that, such as an impact dynamic. I admit it could affect the angle of attack of an iron (i.e., the later you release the more the angle will be descending). But that is so much easier controlled by things like ball position that I am not sure why anyone would ever go there. In any event everybody I've ever heard of "working on their lag" was after distance. I know that's the reason I searched after the "secret" of lag for so many years. It enticed me with the potential for the extra five miles per hour of club head speed that I believed I had to have.

I've done a lot measuring swing speed and videotaping my swing while using various swing thoughts and have noticed only the very slightest rise in swing speeds when the release is slightly visibly delayed. I will give you an example. Two swing thoughts (that appear contradictory) that I often use when I work on my swing speed are:

- Consciously throw the head of club into the ball as fast as I can from the top (sample outcome: club head speeds - 100, 99, 100, 101, 100);
- Consciously slow the left arm into impact and "snap" the lever of the left arm and shaft straight as late as possible (sample outcome: club head speeds - 99, 96, 101, 103, 100). Video shows more quality lag with the "snapping" motion, but only occasionally can I convert it into a higher club head speed. And it is harder to time; for me much harder. Could it be trained over time? Perhaps. Would it be worth changing? I have no way of knowing. Could it actually be harmful? Yes, I think it could be. In my own case I have found much easier ways for me to gain club head speed.

You hardly ever see any studies or even suggestions as to what quantitative speed gains are possible through "holding" lag longer into the downswing. I did see one anecdotal account that I will share. I won't give you a citation because I found its claims ridiculous. It was an e-book about lag. The author claimed that he took his speed rader device and made five or six swings using his normal swing and topped out at around 100 mph. Then he switched his focus to keeping the weight of the shaft in the number three pressure point (he must have read Homer Kelley) and on the next swing, his speed jumped to over 130 mph! I'm sorry, but I cannot believe that happened. I've seen only a few swings in person over 130 mph – it looks nothing like a 100 mph swing. If it did happen, and he wasn't expecting it, it would have jerked both of his arms right out of their sockets. I've hit a lot of balls with my focus on feeling that number three pressure point through impact and the speed for me is about the same as always. For me the swing thoughts that most often produce the highest, most consistent swing speed is put the head of the club on the ball as fast as I can or make that club head "swoosh" as loud as I can, both of which will usually produce a few extra miles per hour for me, especially if I can combine them with the thought of "soft arms." On video, how does my "lag" appear with these swing thoughts? Not "great", not "poor"- somewhere between Sergio Garcia and Tom Watson in appearance.

To me, Sergio Garcia and Tom Watson now represent a perfectly acceptable range of lag "releases." Both are relatively small men who are or were long hitters in their eras. Could Mr. Watson have gotten a little longer by working on delaying his release? Maybe yes. In my opinion, maybe one or two miles per hour of club head speed. Would it have been worth it considering the difficulty of changing the pattern of his release? Probably not.

For most people, I think lag is not worth worrying about. Some people (mostly beginners but a few experienced players) have such an early release that they cannot generate adequate club head speed (I address these in the chapter on Gross Motor Issues). If you fall in this category then you need to examine your swing with a video camera and come up with drills and swing thoughts to remove the pattern. For me, lag was a red herring. The really nice thing about recognizing this is that I can free my mind from esoteric questions such as what part does the lower body play in enhancing the lag. Now when I need club head speed, the only swing thoughts I need are to swoosh the club head as loud as I can while allowing my arms to remain completely soft - they're spaghetti. With those intentions, my lower body moves exactly as it should. If my subconscious mind chooses to do that by lagging the club head just a bit deeper into the downswing, then so be it.

# CHAPTER 11

## IS "COMPRESSION" REPLACING "LAG" AS GOLF'S NUMBER ONE MOST MISUNDERSTOOD TERM?

If you have watched any golf on television at all in the past twenty-five years, you have undoubtedly heard multiple variations of the following: "Wow, that Lydia Ko (or whoever) really compresses the ball"; "He is so powerful – it all come from his compression"; or "You know, the difference between the tour players and the average players is how well the tour players compress the ball." You might even go so far as to say that to much of modern golf instruction "compression" has replaced lag as the secret to golf. Honestly, I am completely sick and tired of hearing golf's talking heads marvel about compression and the good player's ability to apply it. You may be sick of them too.

So I decided to do a little research and see if they actually knew what they were talking about. I looked into what all the top teachers on YouTube said about compression. What I found astonished me – in large part they either didn't know what they were talking about or didn't have a comprehensible way of explaining it. One thing that they all had in common was the belief that attack angle (at least with an iron) was an important portion of compression as was forward shaft lean. I disagree. I will tell you why. Then I will tell you why it is crucially important to designing our golf swings to understand why.

To start with, we need to understand exactly what happens when the face of the club meets the ball. Here's a layman's best attempt at a definition. At impact, the ball "compresses" or flattens against the face of the club. And quite a bit - we see that in stop action photography. The face of the club also actually compresses also against the ball (but just a little). This compression (flattening) reflects a transfer of energy. The more the ball compresses into the club face the greater the transfer of energy (and thus ball speed when it springs off the club face). The factor which, as far as I can tell, exclusively determines the amount of energy transferred to the ball (and the amount of compression against the face) is the quality of the strike, which is completely controlled by sweet spot contact. In other words, our maximum compression, and therefore ball speed comes when the ball is struck right out of the center of the sweet spot (assuming the same club head speed). As contact moves away from that sweet spot in any direction on the face, then that amount of compression and ball speed goes down. Another way of saying it might be that the "smash factor" (optimum about 1.50 with a driver) is reduced. Smash factor just demonstrates the relationship between swing speed and ball speed (i.e.; assume a player swings his driver at 100 mph and gets a ball speed of 150. His smash factor is about 1.50 and we can assume he probably hit it pretty much right out of the sweet spot).

Now, let's think of these considerations in terms of what our YouTube instructors express or imply about compression. That is, that "compression" is improved by a little steeper angle of attack. For example, let's assume a six-iron hit with a six degree angle of attack and one with a three degree angle of attack, both, right out of the sweet spot and at the identical swing speed. The implication to me is that these instructors believe that the ball hit with the six degree attack is better compressed – that is, that the ball would be flattened a little more against the face and come off the face with a little more ball speed. Sort of a little turbo booster of ball speed? Sorry, I can't find any data to support that there is such a boost. The amount that the ball is compressed on the face is the same in both examples, as is the ball speed.

I think I understand what the commentators are talking about when they are talking about compression: they are observing that one method of controlling trajectory and ball flight that good players often, even usually use, is by controlling attack angle (through forward shaft lean). It appears to produce extra power (ball speed) but really is only changing attack angle (and thus launch angle).

So, why do I bring this up about compression? Two reasons, both of which I believe are tremendously important if you are going to remake your own golf swing under your own guidance. First, it is a warning. Consider every source you can for ideas, but examine it very warily, even challenge it. Your time is too valuable to waste on speculative and unsupported theories. Can the source explain clearly what they want you to do and why? With a little research and common sense you can almost always come up with solutions for your own game better than the "experts" can.

Second, I believe that touting superiority of the hands-forward swing is dangerous to our own creativity in creating our own golf swings and our own flexibility in creating our own ball flights and trajectories. Sure, it is one way to do it, and something we should certainly experiment with and understand. Is it the best way? I don't know, but I think great ball-strikers recognize that there are a variety of ways to get great results. I think we recognize this innately.

Let me give you an example from when I was a kid. We knew all about forward leaning shafts – we were taught to hit down on the ball and we saw big divots dug out by tour players. So all of us on our standard iron shots had forward leaning shafts at least to some degree. In those days my top carry distance for a 7-iron was 154 yards off the ground. But we all knew we could get a little more with a simple adjustment. Here is how it worked and as far as I know it works for everybody. We're on a par three. We need to carry it 158 yards but we don't want to hit a soft six. We all knew we could take the seven and tee it up a little extra, move it up a little in the stance and swing at like we were hitting a driver. It works amazingly well. It has the same ball speed (I assume), but comes out higher and has plenty of spin. Does it spin as well as the lower trajectory "standard" shots? Probably not, but we never had to worry about the ball not spinning enough; it stopped fine (of course you can go too far with it at a certain point it could get too high and not get maximum carry). Remember, there were a lot of old school players who liked to play with less forward shaft lean than that employed today by tour players. They liked to take the thinnest divots they could (Moe's "bacon strips" or some even no divots at all). The ultimate example would be Count Yogi who I mentioned in the Foreword. Obviously, I never saw Harry Frankenberg (Count Yogi's given name) strike a golf ball in person. But, by all accounts from those who did he was an exquisite ball striker. He claimed to hit up on every shot, even his irons, and taught his students to never take a divot intentionally! If you will take a look at some of the few videos on YouTube of Yogi hitting full shots you will see a full, flowing, relaxed, and even, to my eye, majestic motion. He is also said to have been a powerful driver of the ball in spite not being a large man. But there on the videos you'll see that cupped left wrist, "flip" and vertical shaft at impact. A better option? I don't know but it is an option that is worth exploring particularly if you don't produce tour level club head speeds. Your optimum trackman numbers for any given shot will be completely different for someone whose swing speed is ten percent or more higher than yours. Blindly following anybody in golf, even tour players, stifles creativity and may gravely harm your golf swing.

I'll suggest one final example of the absurdity of the notions of "compression" that permeate the golf teaching industry. I recently received in my email another solicitation from the Moe Norman Golf Academy. The instructor opined that Moe achieved his superior "compression" by always having his hands ahead of the club head at impact. So I looked up and found the clearest stop action video I could of Moe at impact. It was of Moe hitting a driver at impact and the shaft was vertical and his hands and club head were in a straight line. Then I looked at the impact positions of Jamie Sadlowski and Jason Zuback, two of the legends of long drive: their hands are significantly behind the club head at impact as they launch the ball higher. Is it possible they didn't get the right instruction on "compression?"

# CHAPTER 12

## HOW DAVID TOMS AND TRACKMAN SOLVED MY FIFTY YEAR "SWING" PROBLEM

When I was twelve and learning golf, I was a small, slight kid. My arms were also relatively short – my "levers" were not long. I never grew out of that. It's not surprising then that I would struggle for length relative to the larger players whom I competed with. Everything else being equal bigger players normally hit it further. That's no surprise to anyone. Over the years I tried to make up for it through better "technique", improved "lag", better fitness, etc. The results were unsatisfactory and led to a lot of frustration. The problem was always with the driver and what I thought I needed - ten or fifteen more yards of driver carry (later, as we started measuring such things I started assuming the need to be about five more miles per hour of club head speed). I knew I could get a little more speed with a longer driver shaft and had maxed out at what reasonably worked for me a couple of years ago at forty-six inches (actually a fairly common stock length today). My club head speed with the driver was in the low 100s and my driver carry was in the 235 to 240 yard range that I thought was, as always, a little unsatisfactory. I was in my late fifties but still reasonably fit. I also knew that my driver spin rate was too high for optimum carry — up over the 3000 revolutions per minute range.

Then one day well after the trackman information had become public, I was looking at some tour statistics. According to these statistics David Toms driver swing speed in the low 100s, but his driver carry average was around 270 yards! I was floored. I was not sure that that was even possible (assuming conforming C.O.R.). I knew if I nutted a 100 mph driver, it might carry 240. Now, Toms is not a long hitter, maybe one of the shortest on the tour, but he was figuring out a way to maximize his technique and his equipment. So, with the help of a golf professional where I practice, Walt Chapman, we got use of a Flight Scope launch monitor and an assortment of driver shafts and heads and set to work. It was obvious we had to get the spin numbers under control and to maximize the launch angle. The spin numbers fell dramatically by moving to a lower loft specially weighted low spin driver head. We tested a variety of different shafts until we found a fifty-five gram one that lowered it even more, but bumped club head speed and ball speed up at little also. It settled around 2200 revolutions per minute. I also had to keep the launch angle up. Now I try to get it around fourteen degrees, so with a nine degree driver I have to hit it up on the ball 4 or 5 degrees to do so. The only way that I personally can do that without making a drastic swing change is to move it forward in my stance a little and tee it up on a four inch tee. It looks a little funny but it works for me. I haven't figured out how to get a 270 carry yet, but a 250 carry is very doable without much increase in club head speed or ball speed. I'm sure you are not interested in my trackman driver numbers, but I mention this only to stress the utter importance of equipment and the use of the trackman information to get it absolutely perfect for your swing. The pros do it. It is even more important for you if you have a need for additional distance.

I carry a portable launch monitor with me now when I practice. It really gives me great feedback and it sells under $200.

It seems to accurately measure club head speed and ball speed (and computes smash factor) with numbers very consistent with a $30,000 actual Trackman device. The device I use seems to estimate carry distance a little long often with the driver - I speculate that the device has no capacity to measure spin rate and is calibrated to "optimize" that estimation. One thing that the device is particularly useful for is in comparing your swing speed from one day to the next or even one year to the next.

Equipment is unbelievably important to your golf game. You will have to figure out what works best for you. To maximize it, you will have to take advantage of the trackman technology. Do not blindly trust what the experts tell you. I suspect that sometimes the technology is used to sell clubs. Hit all the demo clubs that you can. Hit your friends clubs. Hit your wives clubs. Very often what optimizes your golf game is contrary to standard. I now have a "stiff" shaft on my driver and "senior" shafts in my wedges. It is what works and feels best for me. To play your best I really believe you should fall in love with your golf clubs. But don't be afraid to experiment. Remember, both Moe Norman and Ben Hogan experimented continually with their equipment until they got exactly what worked for them.

# CHAPTER 13

## HOW TO DESIGN YOUR OWN GOLF SWING

If your interest is peaked by anything you have read so far, you may want to get started designing or redesigning your own golf swing. I can't tell you exactly how to do it. Based on my own experience you will learn much more from and profit much more from the a self-discovery process. I will give you some suggestions, though, that might speed the process. Dumbing it down for myself, I have divided these suggestions into two groups: (1) Pre-swing concerns (including grip, stance, posture, ball position, etc.), and (2) Swing thoughts – mental images and thoughts that you can use during your actual swing to trigger your subconscious mind to create workable golf swing movements. I will consider pre-swing concerns in this chapter and swing thoughts in the following.

- PRE—SWING CONCERNS

Obviously your subconscious cannot re-invent the wheel on every golf shot. Actually it could but the results would likely be very disturbing. It wouldn't make sense to stand to the ball with a completely different grip and set-up at every shot. Your subconscious hones the skill of sweet spot contact and creating the right impact alignments through consistency in the grip and set-up positions. You need to decide upon a group of grip and set-up features that will be most workable for you.

How do you do this? I believe comfort and experimentation and a careful consideration of the athletic task you are getting set-up to perform — making a powerful, athletic sidearm throwing motion at a distant target (at least on full shots). But before you jump into how to go about formulating your own personal grip and set-up guidelines, I think the first thing you should do is take some time – considerable time – to understand as much as you can about the trackman laws. Read every book you can about it. Study everything you can about it on YouTube videos, especially the Joseph Mayo Trackman Maestro videos. Mr. Mayo has a way of explaining some very technical information in an understandable manner for even non-technical people. This information is the only real hard science we have about the how the golf ball reacts with the club head. It explains why the golf ball moves as it does. Don't believe me (believe the PGA and LPGA pros who are using the information to understand and improve their own swings). Trust me. This information will and is revolutionizing golf instruction.

Not only should you understand as much of the trackman information as you can consciously, but I believe it helps to also try to burn it into your subconscious as you study it. Try to visualize as much as you can how the club head and ball look at impact as the ball spins in different directions off the face on different trajectories. I don't think you will ever regret this attention to this supremely important detail. Jack Nicklaus and virtually all other great ball-strikers allowed their subconscious minds to control ball flights with faulty information about the ball flight laws. Imagine what would have been possible if their subconscious minds had been fed the correct information.

After you understand as much of the trackman information as you can ( I call this "what we're trying to do to the ball") I think it is crucial to conceptualize some of the different ways the human body can be used to to achieve impact alignments that are compatible with our trackman intentions. Not all the ways — that is way too complex to understand. But just the simplest ones that through observation seem apply to all golf swings. I believe it is crucial. Obviously, before we try to establish the pre-swing parameters we should have a clear picture in mind of exactly what we will be asking our body to do. I believe that providing the simplest but most accurate picture of what we want our body to do for the subconscious mind to digest and creating a set-up that encourages the simplest way for your body (including the arms) to move is the quickest way to improve your golf swing.

The most crucial idea or concept that I believe you should digest and completely understand is what I will call "squaring the club face to the target line" (not to the plane or path, but let's use trackman reality and think about the actual target line). There are two basic and very simple ways that the body and arms can achieve this and do it in virtually every human golf swing. I would like you to separately experience both of them right now. Seriously. Don't just sit there and think about it. Actually experience it. Get any golf club (except a putter) and stand comfortably face on in front a full length mirror with your feet spread so that your ankle joints are roughly under your hip joints. Take the grip in your left hand in a manner that allows the back of the left hand to point in the same direction as the club face. Put the right hand on the grip so that its palm faces the left hand palm. Now, just move your arms back so that your hands are just in front of your right thigh. From your view your hands should be just over the toes of your trail foot, the shaft parallel to the target line. The toe of the club can be straight up or slightly facing the ground. Let's call this, for lack of a better term, the "delivery position." From there without doing anything at all with the arms-hands unit simply turn your torso (hips and shoulders together) to face the target. If you are like everybody else I've ever seen do this drill I think you'll find that through the impact area the club face squares up by itself very nicely. A wonderful bonus of using the body to square the club face will be apparent if you repeat this drill several times - the club approaches the the ball on an inside path, squares up nicely and exits back inside. If you have a true over-the-top issue (further considered in a later chapter), using the body to square up the club face while leaving a soft arm-hand unit alone will very likely quickly solve it. I think that on video you can find three great ball-strikers who most clearly use this "face-squaring through body rotation" technique: Lee Trevino, Jordan Spieth, and Ben Hogan.

There is obviously another way to square the club face. I call this "forearm rolling." It has been taught, tried, experimented with, criticized, but sometimes even extolled, for I suppose five hundred years. Here's how to separate it out and examine it right now. Get back in front of the mirror, take the same grip as above and move into that same delivery position. Now, this time leave your body alone (leave it facing the mirror) and square the face using only using your arm-hand unit. You will see that the only way to square the face in the impact area is to begin a process of rolling the trail forearm over the lead forearm in the hitting area. I believe that all full golf swings have some degree of forearm rotation with the exception of those where the player consciously or instinctively tries to hold off the that rotation through impact — you may have seen good players do it to stop the club face closure. But at some point in the swing (hopefully after impact for most of us) that forearm rotation naturally occurs without conscious thought; in fact it is very tough to retard. The forearm rotation is the result of the physical forces exerted on them by the weight of the club head on the end of the shaft moving at 100 hundred miles per hour or so.

To get the feeling of that natural forearm rotation and conceptualize it I suggest you take a club and go outside and with soft arms and the grip used in the "squaring the face drills" above and make some full practice swings with no intent to square the face. You will find (assuming soft arms and no intent to hold off the rollover) that they roll over quite fully. There are a couple other things about that rollover that you should note. When the natural forearm rotation occurs, it normally occurs quickly (my strong preference is that it occurs well after the impact area). It is not gradual - the club face flashes shut. If you are going to use conscious forearm rotation as your primary mechanism for squaring the face you had better get used to some very, very long practice sessions. Your timing will have to be exquisite and well-trained. It can be done, but I would ask myself: "At what price?" In addition, you will find that if you examine video of great players that the stronger the rotation of their torsos to "face the target" (or better yet face left of the target), the later that flash of forearm roll will occur. Dustin Johnson's swing from a down-the-line demonstrates this very well today, as did Trevino's and probably best of all Hogan's (from the down-the line view consider how quickly his arm-hand unit disappears from view prior to any forearm rollover).

For you to create a golf swing that allows you to most easily create the the right impact conditions (specifically club face alignment) I believe that you must first decide on how you want to conceptualize how you want your body and/or arms to square the club face at impact. I believe that it is the most important concept by far toward golf shot accuracy (obviously path is also important but I think you will find that very often if the face is correct the path will follow). As I see it you have three choices (in my opinion one fantastic, one poor but at least conceivably workable and one perfectly acceptable) :

- (1) You could decide to be a a face-squarer through pure athletic body rotation (i.e., Hogan, Trevino, Dustin Johnson, and Jordan Spieth). If you are worried that you won't be able to draw the ball if you choose their methods, don't be. The best information we have to date is that whether the ball fades or draws (or goes dead straight) is dialed in with the club face/club path dynamics at the instant of impact). The rate of closure of the face at that instant has no effect, or virtually no effect, on the spin. If you are worried you might be giving up power, don't be — there is no empirical evidence that actively rolling the forearms adds anything to club head speed.

- (2) You could decide to be a pure forearm roller. I can't think of a single good player that is anywhere close to a pure forearm roller, but that affliction seems very common among poor players throughout the ages. You see it everywhere on driving ranges. If your conception of how to square the club face is with forearm rotation then I believe your subconscious mind will respond by over-utilizing the upper body, under-utilizing the lower body and your overall concept of the golf swing will not be an athletic, full-body sidearm throwing motion to a distant target but rather an upper body striking motion at a near target (the ball). [One thing that is unfortunate is that for ages temporary band-aid tips have been suggested to fix what in reality are club face and club path issues. You may have heard this one given to the slicer who can't square the face - just try to hit the with the toe of the club. Not only does it rarely, if ever, produce satisfactory consistent results, but it implants in the mind of the the unfortunate victim that forearm rolling is the best or only way to square the club face.].
- (3) You could decide to be a body-rotation, forearm-roller blend. Many, perhaps even most, good players in the history of golf are blends to some degree. In fact, I believe the vast majority of all golfers are blends whose swings lie somewhere between the two extremes. In my opinion, the closer you lie to the rotator end of the spectrum the more consistency you'll have in squaring the club face and the less you'll have to rely on timing between the lower body and the forearms to get the face square. But, a great player who appears to lie closer to the roller end of the spectrum is Phil Mickelson (maybe a source of inconsistency?), so it is

certainly workable. If you are interested in studying where the golf swings of tour stars lie on that spectrum I suggest you examine some clear slow-motion video on YouTube and check where the fingers of their glove hands first appear below their trail hands in their follow-through's. If it is below their belt line I would place them toward the roller end of the spectrum (Mickelson); if above I would place them toward the rotator end (Zach Johnson). At the highest end of the spectrum you'll find Jordan Spieth (his glove hand fingers don't appear until up around shoulder level). Of course, I classify him as a pure rotator (and pure ball-striker).

In this first step of your journey to design your own golf swing I believe you should first determine which of these three concepts for squaring the face you will adopt. It will greatly assist you in determining your pre-swing fundamentals of grip assembly and stance (which in my opinion are most easily adopted and analyzed as a combination of body posture and body alignment). Once you pick one of these three options I strongly suggest you stick with it for at least as long as it takes to understand exactly why it's not working if it doesn't immediately help. If you have long-engrained club face and club path issues you will be unlikely to see instant results. Be patient there in the beginning. Don't abandon your concept, assume it won't work, and head into another concept or on the the newest golf swing "methodology." I'll give you an example of the wrong way to do it and actually something that is very common. Let's say you decide you want to be a pure body squarer like Hogan or Jordan Spieth. You find your own grip assembly and stance. You feel like you've got your club face alignment perfect for you and you begin hitting full shots. You set up to hit a draw. You can visualize the path of the club head through impact as two degrees in-to-out and the face one degree open to the target line. You feel like you've made a full body rotation and your body rotation just slung your arms through impact. The ball starts out on line but tails to the right. You try another one - same result. The overwhelming tendency is to think: "Well, I can fix that - I'll just roll roll my forearms a bit." And it might, and likely could, work; at least for a while. But now you've transformed yourself back into a blend. You're back to square one. I'll suggest a better alternative - figure out for yourself exactly why that ball wouldn't draw back. I can think of three easy possibilities to consider. One, did you hit the shot out of the sweet spot? If you significantly missed it the normal trackman data relationships and ball flight laws go out the window. If you struck it towards the heel that may have caused some or all of the failure to get the draw spin. Are you confident of your club face alignment at address? I believe it is by far the most important indicator of where the club face will be at impact. If left alone our subconscious minds have an uncanny ability to somehow calibrate and return the club face to its address position. Think about how easy it to pop that impact bag flush every time without thinking about it (or Henry Cotton's tire). But, what if you "addressed " the impact bag with the a different club face orientation each time - it gets much tougher to get that flush "whack" sound of the bag each time. So check to see that the face alignment was right for you (and in line with the principles we discussed previously in Chapter 3). I think you can get "sloppy" some set-up issues and get away with it, but setting the club-face at address perfectly for you is not one of them. Third, was your body rotation active enough? The great body-rotators rotate their torsos very, very aggressively - hips, shoulders, everything. If you've been an arm-swinger for a long time you may be surprised, even shocked at how aggressively. Check in a mirror with an impact bag to see if your rotation is similar.

Once you've chosen your concept for squaring the face, you will want want to marry it to to the grip assembly (which, in my judgment, includes the process you go through in placing your hands on the grip, how your fingers and perhaps palms sit and feel on the grip, as well as whether your lead wrist is cupped, flat or even conceivably arched just a bit as the properly soled and aimed club head sits behind the ball at address with each individual club). Once you've chosen a grip assembly the next obvious step will to be to marry that to an athletic stance which, in my judgment, is best viewed as a combination of posture, alignment of body sections, and arm hang (another way of saying distance from the ball).

The following two sections deal first with grip assembly and then with stance from the viewpoint of the needs of the player who decides upon either the purer rotator or blended conceptions of how he or she wants to square the club face. I believed when I began writing this chapter that virtually no one would select the option of being a pure forearm roller. I do not believe that the same considerations in the next two sections would apply to a pure roller since it would require taking the legs and the torso turn out of the equation.

I started to omit any discussion of what pre-swing options a pure roller might face. Then I realized that I had seen a good ball-striker who was without question a pure roller. I saw him in the nineties at a trick shot exhibition at the club where I was a member. His name is Dennis Walters. This courageous man was an aspiring golf pro who was injured in a golf cart accident in the seventies and paralyzed from the waist down. But rather than wallow in self-pity he kept going with the game he loved. He taught himself to hit golf balls and trick shots strapped and seated on the side of a golf cart. His legs are completely immobile and obviously his swing employs only upper body action and is almost completely without a rotational element. When I saw him in the nineties I only saw him hit drivers. He hit good solid playable draws that each carried well over two hundred yards — he did appear strong in the upper body. Any player, assuming a golf course of a reasonable length, could certainly play excellent golf with the golf swing that the inspirational Mr. Walters had developed for himself. So I looked up Mr. Walters on YouTube and he's still out there performing his show all across the country. He looks older now, obviously - but it appears to me that he still hits his driver as far if not further than other able-bodied reasonably flexible golfers of his age. When I saw the videos of his show it reminded again of a couple of things - first, the title of this book. Because of his circumstances Mr. Walters was required to do exactly what I'm suggesting the reader to do. He rebuilt his own swing. There is no instruction manual out there on how to hit a golf ball if you can't stand up. Second, I realized that the system or conception of the golf swing which Mr. Walters worked out for himself might be instructive or very helpful for a large number of golfers (particularly those with lower body movement restrictions, little interest in lots of practice time, or simply a less complicated way to play golf). Finally, I realized that Mr. Walter's model swing is very much like the option I suggested in my prior short e-book, Lag and the Economical Golf Swing, which I know to be very workable and accurate, if not the most powerful and athletic. Accordingly, at the conclusion of this chapter I will include a brief section suggesting some grip assembly and stance options for anyone interested in a pure roller option. I am viewing video of him to help me in formulating my suggestions and I dedicate that section to him in appreciation for his great inspiration to golfers everywhere.

1. The Grip Assembly at Address.

Since the time that I realized that I needed to abandon all traditional golf instruction and with the help of the trackman information develop my own personal golf swing fundamentals I have discovered, or more accurately perhaps, stumbled across, three realizations about the golf swing and virtually all existing instruction, that absolutely stunned me. The same things about each these three realizations were stunning to me — that they were all obvious to a really careful observer ( I know, I should have recognized them earlier myself), that they are virtually never mentioned or appear in the incredibly overwhelming mass of golf instruction that exists, that the simple appreciation of these three realizations would be extremely beneficial to myself or anyone else seeking to find their own way in the golf swing, and that common sense application of them to one's golf swing might remarkably improve it. In fact, these three realizations are the cornerstones of what I used to "reinvent" my own golf swing and that I thoroughly recommend that you consider when creating or rebuilding your own. It is also fascinating to me that the beneficial use of the three realizations all occur either before the club moves away from the ball or very shortly thereafter. Nicklaus is reported to have said something to the effect that "it's all over within the first two feet." I think I may have a sense of what he was talking about.

The first realization was the information relayed in Chapter 3 of this book regarding club face alignment at address. The second realization I call the "genius of golf club design" and means to me that if the player will let the design of a properly designed and fitted golf club be their guide it very well might lead him or her right into a their own perfect grip, set-up and swing. This will be explored in Chapter 22 as a jumping off point for your experimentation. The third realization is that the isolated consideration of how the hands are placed on the club at address (the unfortunate extent of traditional golf instruction about that unbelievably important subject) is virtually worthless unless it is combined with precise information of what I call the whole grip assembly (hands, wrists, arms, shoulders, lean of the club shaft, and aim of the club face) both at address and at the player's desired impact position.

To get started in your quest to find your own your own perfect grip assembly, I suggest you examine from a face-on view the address positions of the following four great ball-strikers — Hogan, Moe Norman, Knudson, and Trevino. Consider the difference in the appearance of the arm-shaft relationship in each address. With Hogan and Knudson you have what I call a "Capital Y" address — club shaft vertical, or nearly so, butt of the grip pointing at the belt buckle, concave left wrist, and the shoulders closer to level. With Moe and Trevino you have what I call the "lower-case y" address — substantial club shaft lean, much flatter left wrist, straight line of shaft and left arm, butt of the grip points at left hip joint or just inside it, and considerably more shoulder tilt. I'm not sure why golf instructors or theorists seldom mention these obvious differences. Maybe they think "the starting position" is irrelevant as long the player gets back to impact with the right club face, club path, shaft lean,etc. to hit produce the intended shot. In a sense that's true, but I fully believe that that's "doing it the hard way." If you have a copy of Five Lessons handy please look at the illustration on page 42 where Hogan demonstrates what I would call the Capital Y arm-shaft arrangement at address — the butt of the club points right at his belt buckle on a standard five-iron shot. Then turn to pages 102 and 103 where Hogan demonstrates his preferred impact position — the entire grip assembly is now markedly changed, you could even say remarkably changed. And it's not just a "lower case y" now but an exaggerated version of one. I presume the biggest changes are in the leading, supinating left wrist with the raised wrist bone. It is at least six inches more toward the target than it was at address. I don't know much about human anatomy but I do know that the movements of the human hands, wrists, forearm bone, elbows, and even shoulders can to some extent alter the club face aim or angle and all of which have to be controlled by our subconscious mind at lighting speed. The movements are staggeringly intricate. To me it seems like a fine motor skill, kind of like brain surgery or safe-cracking being performed at one hundred miles per hour. Everybody I've ever seen make a backhanded striking motion to a precise target (say a small hammer and a tack) will "address the tack" with their hand, wrist, arm assembly in a position as close as they can to get it to where they anticipate it will be at "impact with the tack." I think it may be instinctive. And the same is true if a corresponding forehanded hammering motion was being made with the trail hand. Why wouldn't a golf swing be similar? Why would Hogan make "aiming his instrument" more difficult for himself?

I think the answer may lie in the history of golf. Hogan came along in a great period of transition in golf — the movement from hickory to steel shafts and the movement from unirrigated muni "fairways" to the soft turf of plush country clubs. I doubt that anyone playing off that brick-hard dirt with a hickory shaft had much interest in a four-inch forward swing bottom. Virtually all of Hogan's famous predecessors (Jones, Hagen, Vardon, etc.) set their shoulders, arms, hands and wrists in that Capital Y formation. But they were pickers, not diggers. That was the style and they were previewing their desired impact positions. But by the fifties perhaps conditions and equipment were more conducive to more forward shaft lean. Hogan was obviously aware of it and sought it, but apparently didn't see the need to change the Capital Y formation he had grown up with. But I do think it would be interesting to know exactly what Hogan meant he purportedly said to John Schlee that "if he could do it all over again he would set up in his impact position." I doubt that he meant that he would set up with his hips forty-five degrees open and and his shoulders thirty degrees open (or whatever the appropriate numbers would be) — it makes it really tough to get any body rotation on the back swing. But, get in front of a mirror and experiment with setting up your whole grip assembly unit in Hogan's desired impact position, maybe just as a drill. It looks a lot like Trevino at address and it forces a great torso turn on the downswing without any thought if you want to be a pure rotator. I'm not sure what Hogan meant in his comment to Schlee but I believe it is certainly possible that he meant that he would have would set up with his whole grip assembly in a "'little y" position that might very much resemble the positions of Moe Norman and Trevino from face-on.

What about George Knudson? He set up with a beautiful Capital Y address. He was admittedly a Hogan fan and borrowed much from him. Video of him shows plenty of shaft lean at impact, but not as much as Hogan. But he was not an old school picker. His left wrist at address is concave, but not as much as Hogan's. With regard to how he squares the club face at impact, he appears to be a clear blend that would sit in the middle of the spectrum between a pure rotator and a pure forearm roller — his body rotation is no where as aggressive as his his idol Hogan. I don't advocate completely modeling anyone's golf swing or methodology, but if I had to pick one from of the myriad of systems that I have tried I would pick Knudson's. His Capital Y set-up is wonderfully symmetrical — his shoulders are virtually level with with each other, his hands are right in the center of the "Y" and the butt of the club points at his belt buckle. His overall set-up appearance is one of complete balance and indeed he considers balance the number one fundamental of his golf swing. Although it is very short and concise with regard to actual instructional content I believe his book The Natural Golf Swing (not to be confused with any of the Moe Norman or Natural Golf schools) is a classic of modern golf instruction.

I believe that Knudson's description of how he places his hands on the club (and just as important the exact procedure he goes through each time he does so) is the simplest and most logical idea out of all the materials I have heard or read about the subject. Whether you consider yourself a pure rotator or a blend I believe that his description provides the perfect starting point for your inquiry. If you believe you might benefit like some of the old school golfers with less shaft lean at impact than the male tour pros use today and prefer to experiment with the Capital Y set-up it might be perfect for you.

Here's my summary of Knudson's ideas about the grip and how I would recommend getting your hands on there the same way every time. You're going to be putting your hands together as in prayer. Holding the grip in the fingers of the right hand sole the club behind the ball with the leading edge perpendicular to your intended start line (using the trackman principles), or based on the principles that were considered in Chapter Three, just a touch right of the intended start line. I can't tell you how much right, you'll need to experiment. Now, this part needs to be done carefully — given the importance of aim in golf this may be the most important part the the whole golf shot procedure. Apply the left hand grip while making sure the the back of the left hand is facing exactly in the same direction as the club face but without altering the club face orientation. Don't be sloppy in this part. Now the back of the left has "become the face." Lee Trevino likes to use the same analogy. Knudson liked his left thumb to run down the center of the shaft and the grip to be in his left palm. It could also be more in the fingers if that's your preference. Apply the right hand, right palm facing the left palm ( the right hand palm has now "becomes the face" too). Knudson felt his right hand was mainly in the fingers. Knudson had the somewhat unusual preference for letting the right thumb run straight down the shaft as well as the left. I believe that utilizing something like Knudson's gripping procedure accomplishes three important goals: (1) it allows the hands to work together instead of against each other; (2) it allows you to marry the club face as well as the intended starting line to the back of your left hand and your right palm: and (3) it gives you a quick simple reliable procedure to lock your aim in on every golf shot you step into. There's no need to try to mimic Knudson's (or anyone's) grip exactly —there's plenty of room for individual preference. But I don't think you could go far wrong if you did.

I suppose if you are a really crazy experimenter, you could explore all sorts of obscure (i.e., cross-handed even on full swings) hand positions that somebody once used or that might be imagined. If that is your ilk, go for it. If not, if you just want a proven playable grip, then I would confine your experiments to a much more limited range - say, the ranges of which have proven workable on the professionals tours, by highly skilled amateurs or even trick shot artists. Given those considerations the grip choices that would leaves you are the traditional Vardon, ten-finger and interlock options. I have tried all three for at least three years each and found that, for me, none made any difference in accuracy or club head speed. I believe like Knudson that it is logical to have your palms face each other. It makes sense to me that to just place hands together in prayer then slide the right palm down the shaft is a very reasonable place to start the inquiry.

Look at the grip described in Five Lessons. If you moved the whole arrangement just a little clockwise around the grip so that you could see three knuckles of the left hand, you might have a pretty standard PGA tour grip. That might be a good place to start. But it could also be anywhere between 1-knuckle (Jose Maria Olazábal) and 4-knuckles (Zack Johnson) and still capable of producing majors winners. I believe that within those parameters the most important concerns are comfort and consistency. Grip changes are very, very hard to make and once the grip is engrained to any significant extent any new way of holding the club will feel strange for a long time. It is very difficult to play decent golf if your grip feels strange or you have any doubts about the "correctness" of your hold on the club. Never, ever make a grip change unless you are absolutely positive of the reasons for the change and your need to do so.

Be very aware of the great danger of relying on these two great platitudes of grip instruction: (1) How many knuckles can you see?; and (2) Where are the the V's pointing to? Those things are going to be highly variable with each individual and dependent on how you set up the whole grip assembly apparatus. Consider a couple of examples. Suppose you like the hand set of of a typical old school player who sets his hands at address with both Vs pointing to his right shoulder and who uses a Capital Y set-up assembly, but you want some forward shaft lean so you flatten the lead wrist toward the target and arch it a bit (essentially moving the whole assembly into a lower case y position). Where do the Vs point now? Or, more importantly what does it do to where the club now face aims? Or suppose you like

Zack Johnson's "four-knuckle" grip but you want to incorporate it into Hogan's Capital Y set-up. So you set up like Hogan on page 41 of Five Lessons with the only exception that you arrange your hands so that four knuckles are visible to you, just like Zack Johnson. Now, move that whole assembly toward the target into that supinating, raised wrist bone impact position that is illustrated on pages 102 and 103 of Five Lessons — you will see that the the face will be remarkably closed and it would impossible to get acceptable club face, club path and attack angles at impact. You will realize that the knuckles and Vs analysis is completely ridiculous if you try to apply to anyone who sets up with any degree of forward shaft lean or raises their wrists to a significant degree. So, why is it used so heavily in golf instruction. I think there are a couple of reasons. First, history is at play again. I'm not sure when it first started (I'm sure it was prior to Harry Vardon), but if you look back at virtually all of the good players prior to Hogan they had very similar looking grip assembly set-ups from face-on — they were virtually all Capital Ys with cupped left wrists and those Vs pointing roughly to their right shoulders ( Sarazen would be an exception with a super-strong grip but he may have made the most aggressive body turn in the history of golf to hold off the club face closure). But, normally from their view, with their cupped left wrists they saw three knuckles. They mimicked each other in their set-ups and were taught that as the proper way to do it. But equipment changed drastically (hickory to steel shafts) as did a move to softer fairways (encouraging more shaft lean). Unfortunately, golf instruction (particularly with respect to the most basic skill in golf — how to best attach your hands to the instrument) never caught up. It is not until Hogan that we see a radically different placement of the hands. And following that obviously enormously important change and the even bigger changes that follow when players begin to flatten the left wrist and build more shaft lean in at address ( see, e.g. Nicklaus, Trevino) traditional golf instruction theorists totally ignore the significance of or consequences of those changes. In my judgment, it is time to completely abandon all consideration of immaterial and long outdated indicia for evaluating your own or another player's positioning of the hands on the club — where the Vs point or how many knuckles he or she can see. I am going to present below an alternative for discovering for yourself a much, much simpler method of attaching your hands to the club (and to organize your entire grip assembly) in a way that you that will enable you to discover for yourself your own grip fundamentals that will allow you to establish the club face, club path and attack angles for your desired shots. You will need a reasonably soft impact bag, something that will work as an alignment rod, a full length mirror (moveable, if available), and your seven-iron to start (I suggest eventually experimenting with it with all of your clubs - it is that helpful and instructive). The drill (or process) is set out below.

- 2. Finding your personal grip assembly

Set up the impact bag against an immovable object such as a pole. You are going to perform a number of fairly sharp one-handed and two-handed strikes of the bag with the club face and it's troublesome to have to reset it after every strike. Place the alignment aid under the bag so that one end of the aid is sticking out in front of where you're standing. That line in now your "target line" (or perhaps the start line of the ball if you are playing a curving shot). The mirror needs to be positioned so that it is perpendicular to the target alignment aid. A point on the bag directly above the point where the alignment aid goes under the bag is going to be your target for the sweet spot of the club. The object of the drill will be to make your strikes as flush as possible. If you've ever experimented with an impact bag you will know immediately when the bag is struck with a perfectly square face — it makes a loud satisfying "thwack" noise. Take a stance roughly parallel to the alignment aid. It doesn't have to be exact. In fact I believe it is actually better to get into the position that you instinctively feel would able to best achieve the assigned task producing that "thwack" noise with left-handed and right-handed swings — for me, that's a little bit open. I suggest a relatively narrow "stance" to start with (ankle joints directly under hip joints) — it allows the body to rotate a little more easily. Set up to the impact bag so that your contact point on the bag is directly above your ball position for that club.

Now take the club in the fingers of your right hand and sole it squarely on the ground behind the bag. It should lie slightly inside the alignment aid and be open to that line. If you have been addressing the ball with a closed club face for a long time you will realize that it looks very, very open. The further you sole the club head behind the ball the more it will be inside the target line and the more open the club face will appear. Envision how that open appearing club face approaches the target from inside the target line and, just as the toe squares up to the heel, produces that loud, satisfying thwack. Now it's time to apply the left hand to the grip and this is the most critical part. With the club head still soled and without changing the orientation of the club face slide the left hand onto the grip while making sure as much as you possibly can that the back of your left hand is facing in exactly the same direction as the club face and the club shaft has the same amount of shaft lean as you would like at impact (what that is for you you will need to decide). For me, I visualize the shaft lean and hand, wrist and forearm positions demonstrated by Hogan on pages 102 and 103 of Five Lessons. It just makes it easy for me to visualize.

Now, make some preliminary left-handed only strikes of the bag with the left arm from the delivery position ( just let the left arm swing back until the left hand is over the right foot and the shaft is parallel to the target line). If you just let the club head follow its natural arc back (it feels like the club remains properly soled for just a few inches) I believe it finds it's perfect delivery spot. From there make some experimental strikes of the bag.

Try to get the bag to make that thwack sound. Just the left arm for now. If you want to be a pure body-squarer make the sole impetus for the strike a nice aggressive torso turn while leaving your arm soft. If you think you want to be a blend between a body-squarer and forearm roller, make it a blend between a torso turn and a left forearm roll. After each strike check in the mirror to see what your shaft lean is at impact and what your left hand and wrist configuration looks like. I suggest you might use the impact configuration demonstrated by Hogan on page 102 in Five Lessons. Experiment with what feels and works best for you to most easily and consistently make that loud whack on the bag and get the right shaft lean. It might be when the grip sits more in the fingers, more in the palm, or some combination thereof. Try it with the wrist flat or a little arched. Who knows, maybe even very arched? Dustin Johnson's might be a perfect model for you. It might be the perfect position for you when the left thumb shaft runs directly down the center of the shaft or perhaps sits slightly behind the center. I believe that within fifteen minutes at the most you can find you own best grip for your left hand — when you do so that perfect thwack will being showing up every time, or almost every time. The great thing about this drill is it also helps in getting the swing path from the inside — with that short backswing you can't make the bag pop if the path is from the outside. Once you are satisfied with your left hand grip, repeat the process with right hand strikes. Sole the club and set the same shaft lean as with the left hand experiments. It could be more in the fingers, or maybe in the palm. Experiment with both. Whichever you are experimenting with in order to get shaft lean there will be some degree of cupping of the right wrist, both at address and impact. Once you've identified your ideal right hand grip put it together with your ideal left hand grip. I believe that if you you will follow this procedure you will notice a couple of important things: (1) That it's not simply a matter of how you place your hands on the grip — you'll realize that the wrists, elbows, shoulders and shaft lean are all important parts of the whole grip assembly; (2) That your new address position grip assembly will be very similar to its impact position ( but there will likely be a little more shaft lean and arch of the left wrist at impact). I believe that the palms of your two hands will likely be facing one another, that the back of your left hand and the palm of your right hand will have become the aimers of the club face. You will have found a grip assembly that you will never want to change again.

- 3. The Body Assembly at Set-up.

Over the last few years I have come to the firm conviction that in all of the areas of human inquiry (including string theory and Chinese metaphysics) there is no area that is more confusing, more convoluted, more contradictory, more bewildering, more over-analyzed, and yet less understood than the question of what is the best way for a player to arrange his body in anticipation of striking a golf shot. Consider just a few of the myriad of variable set-up elements that have been debated over and examined obsessively in published golf instruction and the apparently infinite number of workable arrangements of those elements used by world class players, including:

- 1. Waist bend at the hips or the angle between the thighs and spine (Ben Hogan to Dustin Johnson).
- 2. Alignment with respect or target line of hips, knees, shoulders, and feet (Lee Trevino to Moe Norman).
- 3. Secondary spine axis tilt (Ben Hogan to Lee Trevino).
- 4. Straightness or curvature of of spine (Adam Scott to Jack Nicklaus).
- 5. Knee Bend (Moe Norman to Dustin Johnson).
- 6. Weight distribution (heels, arches, or balls of the feet).
- 7. Distance from the ball and arm hang ( Jim Furyk to Moe Norman) [to which arm length and proportions would appear to be particularly relevant].

- 8. Foot flare (perpendicular to the target line, "duck feet", or some combination thereof).
- 9. Stance width (Moe Norman to Payne Stewart).
- 10. Ball position (one for all clubs or variable).
- 11. Head position, including tilt and eye line.

All of these elements, and many more, have a substantial impact on club face, club path and attack angle at impact. They work together in some amazing, inconceivable combination in the set-ups of all great ball-strikers. To examine each element in isolation, even with respect to one individual, I have realized is absurd. And yet that is what traditional golf instruction and analysis does every day — instructors often isolate and examine each of these individual elements as if they could "stand alone" and even apply as fundamentals to some other, sometimes even all other, golfers as "fundamentals." Even if you could fully understand those relationships with respect to one individual golfer, to attempt to apply them to every golfer, no matter what their size, shape, flexibility, strength, or innate hand-eye coordination is staggeringly absurd.

But, if you are going to discover for yourself your own personal set-up fundamentals you will need a place to start. Trying to sift through, understand, and experiment with the unbelievable mass of golf instruction and workable options that are available, even if possible, would take longer than any human being would ever live. So, in identifying your own personal set-up fundamentals to what source can you turn? I suggest that the easiest, most effective and useful guide will be that remarkable computer inside your head, your subconscious mind. I have come up with a drill, that I will describe in the next section that I use and that has been remarkably effective for me. It will help you find your own perfect set-up. It will look different than mine, and all other set-ups for that matter, but it will be right for you. This drill will help you find all of your set-up elements except for two: distance from the ball and ball position between the feet. But, once you've identified your grip assembly and other body set-up fundamentals those last two can be easily worked out with a little common sense and experimentation.

4. The Set-up Drill.

The visualizations we will use are of how you would instinctively set your body to perform a number of everyday or athletic activities that most resemble the actions of the golf swing. Some occur in reactionary sports. Some are in activities where you have at least a brief moment to "set yourself." They are the actions that most resemble the golf swing — a sidearm throwing or hitting motion to a distant target. I'm sure you've heard of most, if not all of them: skipping a stone across a pond, an infielder making the sidearm throw to first base and the now ancient two-handed basketball pass (both from Five Lessons), the tennis forehand (trail arm) and backhand (lead arm), hitting a baseball (especially as in tee ball), hitting a slap shot in hockey, and actually throwing the golf club down the fairway.

Pick the visualizations that you like best or for activities you are the most familiar with. Or make up your own. Here are the ones I used and I found worked perfectly for me. I was on the driving range and I picked up a ball in my right hand and pretended it was flat stone that I was going to skip across a pond to a distant target. I imagined that I needed to make it skip as many times as I could so it would need some good velocity. I actually made the throw. I didn't try to place my body in any in any particular posture, alignment, stance width or with regard to any of the other body-set up elements — it just happened. My subconscious mind somehow arranged it all for me. I tried it several times. And each time it seemed exactly the same to me — as a bonus the position I was in felt wonderfully balanced and relaxed and perfectly positioned to make that athletic throwing motion to the target. I reasoned that golf is a little different than stone-skipping; that the lead hand is also involved. So I came up with a lead hand analogy: a left-handed frisbee fling at the same target. I tried it several times. Each time the set-up that I naturally stepped into was, as far as I could tell, identical to the others and, in my judgment, very importantly, identical to the one that I had stepped into with the right handed stone-skipping. I knew I had stumbled into something important about my set-up so I went inside and got the impact bag and the mirror went through through the grip assembly procedure set out in section 2 of this chapter and blended my new body set-up with my new grip assembly. What I saw in the mirror was sort of an interesting blend between Hogan's address and impact positions and Trevino's address position. I will describe it only briefly; not as a model but just for general interest. My body alignments ( hips, knees feet) are open (but not as much as Trevino's) except for the shoulders which appear fairly square. My weight is balanced equally between my feet. My stance width is narrower than before — now my ankle joints feel like they are under my hip joints. There is some left foot flare but the right foot looks parallel to the target line. The bend at my hips is a little more than Hogan but not nearly as much as Trevino. My butt seems more under my body and my spine more vertical and naturally curved much more like the old school players than like modern players who have straighter backs, more spine angle and their butts sticking out. My right knee is kicked in just a little, reminiscent of Gary Player. For me, the best thing about my new found set-up is the balance it provides — my weight seems to be distributed not over the heels or arches or balls of my feet but over the entirety of both feet (and equally between both feet). It doesn't feel forced or strained, awkward or contrived at all. Quite simply it feels like it was designed perfectly for me and I arranged myself into it without even thinking. I believe that if you will go through this same or a similar process with the visualizations that seem appropriate for you will find the your own perfect set-up that you can blend with your perfect grip assembly. Maybe the best thing about it is I will never have to think about the set-up again. I'll just imagine skipping the stone and my subconscious moves me right into my perfect set-up.

There are only two remaining set-up concerns to consider: ball position and distance from the ball. I believe they can both be easily resolved once you get your own grip assembly and other set-up fundamentals. I suggest the old tried and true method — with an iron or fairway wood take a practice swing and a shallow thin divot. When you make a swing that feels right check to see where the divot starts and the position for the ball for the that club is just behind where the divot starts. With the driver, because of my distance issues I want to catch it on the upswing so I move it three of four inches in front of where the practice swing bottoms out. With the irons and the fairway woods my ball position is variable between clubs but not as much as I thought it might become (I think because my stance is a little narrower than it used to be). I would suggest that if you are of the single ball position inclination ( i.e., Nicklaus, Greg Norman) you may need to consider more stance narrowing between clubs to keep the swing bottom far enough forward on the shorter clubs.

Finally, with respect to distance from the ball and arm hang, I believe this is the easiest to locate. At least it was for me. Since I am short and stocky I just take my grip and stance assemblies and just let my relaxed arms fall on my chest. Then just a very slight, subtle bend at the waist allows the club head to sole on the ground into what I've found to be the best ball position for me. Of, course that distance gets a little further away with each longer club. I would suggest that in finding your perfect distance from the ball letting your arms lie comfortably on your chest is a good place to start. I also suggest that when you're trying to locate the right distance for you, you might want to run some experiments with some impact tape. If your sweet spot misses tend to be very predominately heel or toe side you might benefit from a slight adjustment by moving slightly closer to or further from the ball. But once you've located your perfect grip assembly, stance and ball position I believe distance from the ball can be quickly discovered with a little experimentation. I believe that comfort will play a large role. You will feel it immediately if you are "reaching for" or "cramped" as you address the ball — your balance that you found when you located your perfect set-up will change a little. I would note that Knudson lined the ball very noticeably off of the toe of the club. We are all different. But Knudson had to find his own way, just like we have to find ours.

- 5) Possible Pure Roller Concerns.

If you decide for whatever reason that you would like to be pure forearm roller I believe you are entering into unchartered territory in golf swing theory. Why? Because the only way to be a "pure" forearm roller is to take the body's rotational element out of the face-squaring equation. I know of no recognizable golf swing theory that recommends that there be no body rotation in the golf swing. But it does have one thing greatly in its favor as a swing theory — wonderful simplicity. Like Moe Norman said often, "My swing's got the least moving parts."

To find your grip-assembly and set-up fundamentals as a pure roller I believe you can still use the impact bag as mentioned above but you should change your visualizations to conform to a different conception of the golf swing motion. Instead of a sidearm throwing to a distant target motion, I suggest a powerful arm-driven striking motion with the lower body providing only a stable base. I suggest setting up to the impact bag and mirror as described in the exercises above but instead of using one of the sidearm throwing motion visualizations try this one: Imagine that the impact bag is the trunk of a big tree. At the target point on the bag there's a spike sticking straight out. The golf club is a heavy sledge hammer and you need to drive that spike in as deeply as you can. With this different intention I think your subconscious will move you into a completely different set-up position. I believe you will naturally take a wider stance and perhaps have a little more knee bend to stabilize moving the heavy hammer. You may find you bend a little more at the hips. With regard to the grip assembly I think you will also find the palms facing each other and the "back of the left hand becoming the club face" principles a great starting place for your experimentation. I think two of the principles that might very well end up being the foundations of such a swing would be that the body never rotates or moves (it just stabilizes) and the address position is identical to the impact position. I suggest further that setting up in a slightly closed stance will "lock-in" in an in-to-out swing path for you at address and you may have simplified the club path variable that faces pure body-squarers and blends. The more body movement you can take out of the swing the better off you will be. A very wide stance as well as a back ball position will help with that and I believe would be a good place to start your experimentation. Also helpful might be to set significant knee bend at address and try to maintain that same knee bend through impact — sort of like a lumberjack swinging an axe.

# CHAPTER 14

## HOW TO MAKE THE MOST EFFECTIVE USE OF A VIDEO CAMERA – USE IT TO SPOT AND ELIMINATE ANY OF THE THREE MAJOR GROSS MOTOR FLAWS

A couple of years ago I got a nice video camera to use in videotaping my own golf swing. When I first started using it, I believed it would lead to startling and revolutionary insights into my golf swing. After all, I assumed, one of the biggest problems we've always had in self-analyzing our golf swings is that we can't normally see ourselves.

At first, I was like a kid with a new toy. I used it every time I practiced my full swing for about a year. I followed the same procedure each time. Before I went to the range, I came up with a swing thought that I would use for the day. I assumed I could see visible changes in my swing based on what swing thoughts I was using. I filmed my practices using that day's swings thoughts and then took it home, downloaded it in my computer and observed the "change." The funny thing is that in that year there were rarely any visible differences. When I looked back after a year, my swing looked the same at the end of the year as it did at the beginning, and in spite of working with probably hundreds of swing thoughts over that time I could never, ever tell what swing thought I was working on in a particular day's video without looking at my notes. I learned a couple of things from my video experience – when your golf swing is as engrained as mine is (what I now call my gross motor pattern) it is extremely difficult to change it. Changing it can be only done though hundreds or thousands of exaggerated repetitions. I hadn't made any change that I could identify in a year, so I eventually gave up on my video camera and I don't plan ever use it again.

However, I think that for some players a video camera might be a very useful, even essential tool for self-analysis. Those are players whose swings, for whatever reason, have what I call gross motor issues. I group these issues into three categories, and if your pattern fits into one or more of the three, you will be unable to generate acceptable club head speed or achieve workable impact dynamics. When I list them, you will likely recognize them immediately because they appear over and over again on every driving range around the world and they are each the subject of volumes of golf instruction. They are the issues that golf professionals address day after day. The three gross motor issues I see are: (1) Not enough backswing length (leading to inadequate club head speed); (2) The very early arm cast (leading to inadequate swing speed); and (3) The over-the-top move (leading to an inability to produce a workable, normally inside-out, swing path). I am not being critical of anyone who has these issues. I have dealt with them before, when I was young, and I had to change my own gross motor pattern to get rid of all of them. I think they are all very common and the last two might even be said to be the natural way that our subconscious minds' use at first to solve the problem of striking a golf ball with power. If you think you may suffer from one or more of these gross motor issues, I believe that the first thing you should do in fixing your own golf swing is simply to address the pattern and change it. I think you can do it most quickly with the help of a good video camera.

How do you know if you've got one (or some combination) of these three patterns? It's likely you've been told by your golf professional, by your playing partners, or you've seen it on video yourself. If you believe that if you are seriously distance challenged, you likely have one or both of the first two issues. If you find it impossible to start a draw to the right of the target line, there is a significant chance you have an issue with the over-the-top (but also likely is a club face alignment at address issue). If I thought I had problem with one of the three major gross motor issues, here is what I would do with my video camera to clearly identify for myself that I had the problem and identify solutions that might help me remove it.

- 1. - Gross Motor Issue #1 - Lack of sufficient back swing length or depth.

Go to your practice area and set up the camera to get a face-on caddy view of some driver swings. After you are sufficiently warmed up, take a piece of tape or other visible marker, and place it on the tip of your left shoulder joint (or forward shoulder). Out on the very tip – on my golf shirts I can feel a little seam there. Tee up a driver with the ball placed in the pretty standard left heel position. Place your video camera across from the ball on a line perpendicular to the target line. Hit some drivers until you are reasonably comfortable that you have demonstrated your normal swing. Now take a look at the playback of your swing and focus on the top of the swing position. Consider these three things: (1) Does your left arm get to at least a three-quarters position (a little elbow bend is fine); (2) Does the marker on your left shoulder get at least a little behind the ball (away from the target); and (3) Is the angle between the shaft and the left arm somewhere around ninety degrees - I know it's tough to tell from that angle. It can be more, or less, but you will have some amount of angle there. There are no absolute rules, but just my opinion, the absolute minimum would somewhere around thirty-five degrees. Think of it this way – the more angle you have there, the more "potential" energy you might have.

If you find video proof of a flaw (particularly with respect to getting the tip of the shoulder marker behind the ball) fix it as soon as you can. How to do that is something you will have to experiment with and discover for yourself. Here are my suggestions. First, these issues are often caused by disabilities and particularly loss of flexibility as we age. Consider yoga, or better yet develop your own flexibility drills to address your unique issues. Second, work with relaxing the tension in your upper body. Tight muscles won't move as far (or as fast) as loose ones. Try relaxing the tension in your arms, your shoulders, and your back. Experiment with a more leisurely backswing. For many people a quick back swing is a short one. Experiment with flaring your right foot out at address and even with dropping it back away from the target line a couple of inches. It will encourage a fuller hip turn and a corresponding bigger shoulder turn. Try instead of just focusing on getting your lead shoulder under chin in the backswing, focus on turning your right shoulder behind your head. Finally, experiment with allowing (I would allow it, not force it) your weight to move fully into the inside of your right hip or heel at the top of the swing while permitting your left heel to rise (like the old-timers – allow it, but don't force it). Also consciously focus on making allowing a bigger hip turn going back — it opens the torso to up for a bigger and deeper shoulder turn. You can even allow the right leg to straighten during the backswing like a lot of the old time players. I've found that when I hit a lot of balls I fall into of making shorter and shorter backswings - sometimes I think we just get lazy about making a full turn. There are many ways to work on this issue – in the back yard, in front of a mirror, at the range. But get it done and verify the results with your video camera. I can't tell you how long it will take to eradicate the pattern. That likely depends on how engrained it is. But, with enough work, you can change it. Work on it until you can get that marker on your lead shoulder three or four inches behind the ball at the top of the swing when you check it with the video camera (making sure that the camera angle is the same as when you first checked it).

Here is one final idea that is definitely worth considering if you struggle with getting you left shoulder "deep" in your backswing. Consider allowing some "head float". Very few world class golfers keep their heads completely still in they golf swings despite that old saw of golf instruction. Perhaps Adam Scott comes the closest. Experiment with allowing your head to float away from the target as your weight loads into your trail heel. If your shoulders are turning at the same time your chin will likely turn away from the target also. If you allow this this happen you may find that you look like a lot of great players at the top of the swing. Your head will have moved back and often even down and your chin will likely being pointing behind your trail foot. The tip of your lead shoulder will necessarily be in a deeper position behind the ball if you can get into this position.

- 2. - Gross Motor Issue # 2 – The Premature Release.

I also recommend the use of your driver to identify this issue and the same camera position as used for Issue # 1. Make sure the camera is set in its best position for good resolution – it's the maximum shutter speed on mine.

Examine what happens to the angle between your left arm and shaft right from the top in the downswing. With many good players it stays about the same. With some players the angle actually gets smaller, which is referred to as "down cock," as in the swing of Sergio Garcia. Either of those is fine. But the one thing you don't want is for that release of that angle to start immediately. Everybody's club releases in a slightly different manner. In my opinion it is not going to help you to try to mimic another player's release. It's too unique – like a fingerprint. I believe that you have a problem with Gross Motor Issue # 2 if you notice from the top a visually significant increase in the angle between the shaft and the left arm prior to the left arm reaching the parallel to the ground position. If you are concerned about this issue at all, please go to YouTube and study video of Tom

Watson and Steve Stricker to check out "early release" patterns that are perfectly acceptable. I would use them as the outer limits for what is acceptable in terms of an early release. So, if you can identify that you have a problem with a too early release, how do you get rid of it? You have entered the mysterious area of "lag" if you're thinking about this issue. There are hundreds of videos on YouTube on how to improve your lag, which is really just another way of saying getting rid of a too early release. With all of the lag drills I've looked at and tried I've found the following to be true: all of them work for somebody at some time; none of them work for everybody all the time. All you can do is try them, experiment with them and see if you can find one or several that work for you, as verified on your video camera. Video the drills with practice swing and full shots. One thing you should look at very soon in figuring how to get rid of an early release issue should be to try to get a really good feel for what lag (the sensation of the club head lagging behind the hands) feels like.

Here is a drill that can really implant that feeling. Grip a club very softly in both hands. Your arms also should be very soft and remain soft throughout this swing. Swing the club back with the hands actually moving first and the club head dragging behind. It is the old "caddy drag" – a look that Bobby Jones and other old time players had. Feel the weight of the club head as much as you can. Don't try to set the angle of the left arm and shaft at the top of this swing. Let the weight of the club head set the angle. If you have managed to keep your arms and hands soft, that angle will set itself and you should feel some pressure in your right hand; your right forefinger to be exact (Homer Kelley's P3). More pressure there equals more lag. By focusing on that P3 pressure point you can quickly learn what you need to do to allow the creation of the lag, to retain it and let it release later. The longer you feel the pressure in P3 coming down, the later the lag will be released. To start with, just make a lot of soft practice swings, leaving that pressure into P3 as far as you can into the downswing. For everybody I have ever heard of, softness in the arms and hands is part of the solution.

I believe that if you struggle with a too early release you will invariably have at least to some degree a misconception about the easiest and most efficient way to increase club head speed. You have a "hit impulse." To whatever extent you have the conception (consciously or subconsciously) that speed is maximized through a muscular arm-striking motion at the ball I believe you should attempt to change that to one of the rotating torso slinging the inert arms into an orbit around the body. All you need to really do is to just leave your soft arms alone from the top. Make absolutely no effort to pull your arms down or drag the handle of the club down toward the ball — absolutely none. Pretend your arms are made of rope. Just let the rope lay across your back at the top and then sling it into orbit with a powerful torso turn. I think that in virtually all cases that too early release will disappear.

- 3. – Gross Motor Issue # 3 – The Over-the-Top.

Like virtually everything else in golf instruction there is no generally accepted definition for the over-the-top motor pattern. I found about a dozen definitions but none that are really suitable to explain it. Prior to realizing the importance of the trackman data, I found the following image to be very helpful to me in describing it. Imagine Hogan's pane of glass in Five Lessons, resting on his shoulders at the top of his backswing (see p.88). Now imagine the slight tilt to the right of the pane as he starts down – it allows the club head to approach the ball from the inside. Now imagine if the pane of glass had instead been tilted left of the target. Then, the club head moves over the pane as it sat at address and could only approach the ball from the outside. That is the move we see most often in players when they first take up the game. Watching them from down the line perhaps the most obvious thing we normally see is an immediate move of the right shoulder toward the target line starting the downswing (and left shoulder moving back from it). The movement of the right shoulder immediately toward the target line is so common that you might even say it is the method most often used by an untrained subconscious mind to deal with problem of hitting a golf ball.

If the over-the-top pattern is not severe, it may be a useful one, sometimes a very good one. Golf swing theorists often suggest that Sam Snead came slightly over-the-top so if the degree of over-the-top is not severe, it may not be a problem at all. Although it is hard to see on video I would suggest that Sam was lining his body up enough right of the target line that he could make a slight over-the-top move and still have a slight in-to-out swing path. When the trackman information first became important to me, I stopped thinking as much in terms of body position and motions and just in terms of swing path (and face angles). I now like to refer to over-the-top as any gross motor pattern which prohibits the player from achieving an in-to-out swing path. So, in my limited definition, Sam Snead would not be "over-the-top" (but his backswing plane could still be under his downswing plane). So, how do you know if you have an over-the-top move that you need to fix? You will be unable to deliver an in-to-out path to the ball (assuming that in-to-out is the swing path that you desire).

Before you set out to fix a suspected over-the-top motor issue there is something very important for you to consider. "Over-the-top" is in my opinion the most misdiagnosed swing "flaw" in the history of golf. You see this misdiagnosis made all the time by amateur instructors, professional instructors, and even the players themselves. The player hits a shot that starts left of the target line. It may continue straight left, curve further left or curve right. The diagnosis is immediately "you came over the top." Prior to the recognition of the trackman data it made perfect sense — "the ball started left and path controls starting line and face controls where it ends up — Nicklaus said that in Golf My Way." What could be more logical? But golf is not ruled by rules of logic, but rather simple physics. As we talked about earlier, now, thanks to the trackman information, we know that more than eighty percent of the ball's starting line is caused by the club face angle at impact. Path does have an influence on starting line, but not nearly as much as the face angle. The practical effect of this information is that in many, many cases where the over-the-top diagnosis is made there is really little or even no path issue at all — the club face was just closed at impact. It can often be simply resolved by just setting the club face more open at address. If you try this there is another phenomenon that I believe is very important to consider. I've observed it in my own experimentation and I've heard it referred to by golf instructors who rely heavily on the trackman information. I call it "path follows face" and I believe that is how the instructors refer to it also. I'll describe how it works for me and most others that I've observed. When a player soles the club behind the ball with the face appearing open to the target line the subconscious mind somehow associates that face alignment with an in-to-out path. And the reverse is also true. If you sole the club behind the ball with the face shut, the subconscious mind tends to match that with an out-to-in path. You might say that you are programming in an over-the-top move by laying the club face down closed to the target line. You might say the subconscious mind prefers to match face angle with path, recognizing that that is the best route to straight golf shots. I don't understand it but I know that that is the way it works for me — the overwhelming sensation I get with it is that the subconscious mind tries to match up the path with the face. Once I was able to recognize this path follows face phenomenon I was able to control path much more easily by just letting the club face lead it. And now thanks to the trackman information and the path follows face phenomenon I can now hit the desirable open faced draw and closed faced fade at least with some regularity. I would suggest that your first step in your over-the-top inquiry might be to try setting the face up more right and see if you can get the ball to start on the line you desire. I hope you won't try to fix an "over-the -top" issue if you really only have a face alignment problem. I would go so far as to say that it may well be that the best "over-the top" cure in the world is simply to lay the face of the club down more open and let your subconscious mind do its work. It would always be the first place I would look in addressing an "over-the-top" issue. And if you start it right and it curves further right, make sure you didn't hit it off of the heel before you deduce that the club face was too open at impact. But, if you still can't get the ball to start on your desired line after you've opened the face at address you very likely do have an over-the top issue that needs fixing.

Again, the video camera can be your best friend in identifying and fixing the problem. Video your swing from down the line; your camera will be positioned directly behind the target line. Your primary focus will be carefully observing how the club head comes into the ball. Try hitting the inside quadrant of the ball. If your swing is significantly over-the-top, you will observe the club head coming into the ball from the outside. Place an alignment marker behind the ball directly down the target line so that you can see it clearly. In virtually every case where it approaches the ball from the outside and you are seeing a true over-the-top you will also see that early right shoulder move toward target line.

How to fix the over-the-top if you identify it? There maybe two hundred over-the-top drills and cures on YouTube. The pattern is that common. As with the lag drills, all of them will work for somebody, sometime, but none of them will work for everybody, at least not all the time. You will have to experiment with them and your video camera. I can offer a few suggestions you might want to start with. First, try a simple one – just try to keep your arms relaxed and hit the inside quadrant of the ball. Allow your back to face the target longer on the downswing – much longer – you can really exaggerate this one. Place a head cover just behind and outside the ball so that if the club head approaches the ball from the outside, it will strike the head cover. Make a track with tees setting up an inside-out track for the club head to approach the ball.

I'm going to repeat what I said earlier what I said about the path follows face concept — how the club head is aligned at address strongly affects the path the subconscious will use through impact for many people. If you have been setting the club face closed at address for a long time club face alignment is definitely something you will want to experiment with. It may take a while to adjust to a club face looking now radically open but your subconscious may eventually adjust and match the face up with an in-to out path without any more "effort" on your part. Here's another thing you might want to look at if you are addressing an over-the-top issue. I have heard several times that early in his career when he was struggling, Nick Price went through a six-month period where on every shot he hit, practice or play, he purposefully dropped his right foot back several inches from his target line. I am not sure what he was working on but it seems to me like it might be a very good method for ingraining an inside-out path.

From a conceptual standpoint there is there is one thing that should be mentioned about the over-the top issue. It is often seen together with the too early release pattern - you could almost say they were twins. I believe they usually occur together because they both result from that same conception (or, in my opinion, misconception) that the easiest way to create club head speed is with a muscular strike of the arms. If that is the case then I suggest that you use the same imagery to change it. Imagine your inert rope arms being slung into orbit by your powerfully rotating torso. You might just kill two very nasty birds with one very easy stone.

One final point about an over-the-top pattern, or at least about how it applies to an in-to-out swing path. It is conceivable that you could decide that you don't care to ever hit the ball with an inside-out swing path (I call this the Lietzke exception). You might conclude that you want to hit only fades (or even slices) — that it is much easier to play and maintain your golf swing with that single left-to-right pattern. That would be exactly what Bruce Lietzke, a very successful tour winner did in the seventies. He was an excellent ball-striker and they say virtually never practiced, at least after his college years. But they also say he never, ever drew the ball or hooked it. When the situation suggested a hook or draw on the course, he just had to figure out some way to play his fade. What would Bruce Lietzke's trackman's numbers look like? I am guessing – for a six-iron (maybe two degrees out-to-in path with a one degree closed face) – for a driver (maybe four degrees out-to-in path with two degrees closed face). If your swing is slightly over the top and you think you could make numbers like that work for you, then I say go for it and ignore this entire section. I doubt Bruce ever wondered whether he was "over-the-top."

# 15

## SKILL DEVELOPMENT FOR YOUR NEW SWING

If you develop your own new golf swing and base its fundamentals on the ball flight laws, which I highly recommend, you will need to feed information into your subconscious with regard to three things (but only three things):

- 1) Face alignment.
- 2) Swing path along with low point central.
- 3) Sweet spot contact.

If you have studied the trackman laws, you will realize that these things are just about all that you need to know. If your subconscious can control these three things, there is not a lot that can go wrong. I believe the majority of your practice time should now go into your training of your subconscious mind's ability to control these three factors. You might refer to this training as skill development. I believe that it makes sense to train each of the three areas separately. I will share with you exactly what I have been doing with my own training. I do not suggest it as something you have to do. Just something that has worked for me.

- 1.- <u>Face Alignment</u>. — Here are a few of my own thoughts on face alignment first. As you have read, traditional golf instruction (leading edge perpendicular to target line) has an inherent and significant issue with accuracy in face alignment (it shades the face left for the right-handed player). Players have compensated for both open and closed club face alignments throughout the history of golf. Because of the remarkable abilities of the subconscious mind, good players, even great players, are able to do something really remarkable. Set the face up at address in what I would call a "less than optimum" position but return it to impact in the optimum position. (see e.g., K. J. Choi – closed at address but square at impact or Steve Elkington – substantially open at address but square at impact). They are obviously workable. But it is my strong suggestion that we make the task as easy on our subconscious as we can. Logically, I believe our brains are able to more easily carry out skills of using striking instruments when the implement is placed in a position at address that most resembles the impact strike position. So with the example of the pool player (straight back and straight though strike) or a carpenter hammer (curved path) the address positions and impact face alignment are identical as possible. Why would you ever want to do it any other way? With my own training I have found that where I set the club address – that's where my subconscious returns it at impact virtually every time. I guess I could foul it up, but I believe I can say that if you can get the face angle exactly like you want it at address our subconscious is very good at duplicating that angle at impact. I work very, very hard on getting it exactly where I want it at address, and I use the magnetic face angle aimer tool to do it. I use it with every club. With my driver the magnet won't work so I tape the device to the face, that pointer coming right out of the sweet spot. Obviously, you cannot hit balls with it. But you can set up to balls and targets with it. Visualize exactly how that pointer comes out of the sweet spot through the ball and down your starting line. It is also very helpful to relate that starting line to a very accurate target line. The best way to do that that I know of is to put an alignment aid in front of the ball directly down the target line to the target [a note on alignment aids: In my judgment the simple alignment stick or aid is the most misused swing aid in golf instruction. I know there are tour pros who use them to align their body sections by placing the stick across their toes, behind their heels, or somewhere in between the foot line and target line. I know all about the parallel left or railroad tracks notion that we should line hips, shoulders, knees and feet all up parallel left. It makes superficial sense — but I believe that in reality it makes no sense. Look from a down the line view at how the all the great ball-strikers "aimed" their hips, shoulders, knees and feet. You will find an amazing variety of the directions in which their body sections point. I believe they weren't aiming their body parts — they were simply aiming the club face and allowing their bodies to naturally set up into positions or alignments that allowed them personally to achieve the right club face aim and path direction at impact, which for them was pretty much straight down that target line. Only Knudson mentions aiming his body, and that is at the target, not the parallel left concept. Quite simply, the only essential things we aim in golf are the club face and to a lesser degree the club path. You may have seen the poor high handicapper standing on the golf course or driving range and placing a club or stick across his shoulders trying to figure out where he should aim them. I've even seen them doing it with the club across their hips. I suggest that that person is misguided with respect to what needs to be precisely aimed in golf. I further suggest that even the tour pro who is using an alignment aid to aim his or her body parts is misguided. When you use an alignment aid, and I certainly believe you should, please use it for its highest and best use: to identify your target line and the relationship between your club face or path and that line.]. Visualize how the pointer should look in relation to your target line with regard to draws and fades. Burn into your subconscious how it looks when you get it aligned perfectly for a particular shot with a particular club. I don't think you need to do this every time you practice. If it's like mine, your subconscious will engrain these new visualizations very, very quickly. Then just practice with your pointer again if you start to get uncomfortable with your aim. Like I said, there are no fundamentals in golf, but if there were one, my choice would be club face alignment at address.

- 2- <u>Face Path (along with low point control)</u> – In the late seventies I read a golf book by Harry Obitz and Dick Farley titled <u>Six Days to Better Golf</u>. There was nothing earth-shattering in their instruction, but there was one little part I have always remembered. In the book was an exercise they called "brushing" that they taught to all of their students. They describe it as follows: "you brush the grass for about six inches going back and again about six inches swinging through." There are a couple of things about their little brushing exercises that I think are interesting. You need a little bit of grass to really get a nice "brush," three-quarters of an inch or so. If you set up with the shaft pretty straight up and down and just sweep the club pretty much straight back and through it will rise a little bit in the backswing, lower back down on the downswing until it reaches its low point (when the shaft is straight up and down again) and then rise up and again on the follow through. As long as you just brush the club back and through the grass with no interference from your conscience mind, it produces a nice little back and forth stroke through impact. When I began working on building my own swing around the trackman laws, I realized that the little brushing technique might be very useful. For example, if you want to ingrain a zero swing path into your subconscious all you need to do is find a area of long fairway grass or short rough, set the shaft perpendicular to the ground, the sole flattened just above dirt and brush back and through. When you want to take a little loft off through impact, you just let the hands lead a little bit coming through. If you want to set up a little in-to-out stroke, you just aim the whole body apparatus at address a little to the right. If you want an out-to-in path, you just set the whole body apparatus left and brush down your body lines. For me, I have come up with a little brush stroke chipping drill I like to play around with in practice (I don't use it playing). I set up to a chip with my seven-iron in longish grass and just brush back and thru, trying to zero out the club path. I set up with the shaft perpendicular and then let my hands lead the club head by a little through impact (so that the low point gets ahead of the ball). I just try to brush back and brush through. There is no need for a divot. I will just try to feel a little straight seven-iron brush chip. Then I will try to brush a little seven-iron draw chip – do the same thing but the body is set up two degrees right and the face one degree right. Then a little cut chip – the body is set two degrees open and face one degree open. As long as the hands are ahead of the club head on the brush through, low point will be in front of the ball. If I want the low point to be even further forward, I will let the hands lead the club head even more coming through. I have been using this little brush through chip practice occasionally for showing my subconscious different club paths for about six months and it works well for me. It seems to bleed over into my full swing and now it has become habituated. Now, when I attempt to hit a draw or fade on a full shot I can just visualize the shot and my subconscious leads me through the set-up and swing procedure. To me, it is almost eerie how well it works and how simple it is to execute once you turn it over completely to your subconscious mind. You may find a better way of feeding club path information into your subconscious, but so far I haven't. Another helpful tool to train club path is to hit balls within one tee behind the ball and one in front on the path you want to ingrain. Move them around for different flights. I find I begin to align my body with the tees and my club face with the starting path. It provides great visual assistance. Finally, you may want to work on your low point control with some divot practice. I like to practice taking very thin divots. The ones I like to repeat as much as I can, are somewhere between a bacon strip and just brushing the grass at the level of the turf.

- 3 — Sweet Spot Contact – Nothing in my opinion, will improve your ball-striking more than training your subconscious to strike it right out of the sweet spot just as often as you can. If you hit everything right out of the sweet spot, your misses would be small and infrequent. You can't over-practice this.The way this skill is normally learned and practiced is with impact tape. It was around even when I was kid. We placed it on the club face and it left a mark on the tape where impact was when you hit a shot. Use it as much as you can afford. It shows you exactly where your misses are on the face. You can see the results of each miss and you will quickly learn to feel the results. Without even thinking much about it you will get better and better at center face contact. We used to get about ten shots out of one piece of the impact tape. After that we couldn't tell much from it. Since the tape was expensive at one point I went with foot powder. That can work well, except when it's wet. Then it's messy. Recently I was at the range where I saw a good player putting duct tape (silver) on the face of his iron. It worked well for him. So I tried it and it works just about as well as the impact tape. And it's a lot cheaper. I saw something recently that might be as helpful as the impact tape. It was a training club, I believe a seven-iron, with rubber (or other non-metal) in the toe and heel areas such that if you significantly missed the sweet spot, it bounced off one of the inserts at a funny angle ( I think normally left if you hit the toe insert and right if you hit the heel insert). Anyway, I think the idea is that your subconscious quickly learns to avoid those inserts and significantly increases your percentage of sweet spot contacts. I haven't tried it but it makes a lot of sense to me. I think you might accomplish the same results with some large size rubber bands around the toe and heel areas of the club face. Finally, here is my favorite sweet spot practice which I use every time I practice or play — auditory and kinesthetic sweet spot practice. I like to hit a lot of sand wedges in the fifty yard range. When I hit them right off the sweet spot, they make a different sound. A nice, clear unmuffled click. I like to hit a lot of them quickly, no thoughts other than just hearing that beautiful sound and solid feel of "perfect impact." I like to use the half-shots because it is so much easier to repeat. I might hit a whole bucket of balls just ingraining that sound and feeling into my subconscious. No swing thoughts are necessary. Sometimes I like to combine it with alternating between little baby fifty yard fades and draws. For the draws the path is set two degrees open, the face one degree open. For the fades it is the opposite. But still the focus on the sound and feel of the sweet spot impact. It is almost mystical how quickly your subconscious gets very good at these little shots. In my case, the improvement in sweet spot contact bleeds over quickly into full shots as well. I fully believe you can get the training work done more quickly with these shorter shots.

Finally, there is one form of skills training that is so useful and in my mind so essential that I mention it separately. It trains all of the most critical elements of impact (club face, club path and attack angle) simultaneously. It is slow motion and half speed training with the impact bag, mirror and alignment stick we mentioned in Chapter 13 and that I encouraged you to use to locate your own grip assembly and body set-up assembly. I would encourage you to set up the bag, mirror and stick just as we did in Chapter 13 and begin by making slow motion practice swings rehearsing how the club head squares up just as it comes into impact from the inside (if that is your intention). Start with small ones (just from the delivery position). Check the mirror each time to get the shaft lean you want. Check your torso rotation rotation if you want to be a true rotator or a blend to make sure your body is fully engaged in the face squaring up. Train your subconscious mind like a ninja or as in other martial arts (or like Ben Hogan did) in slow motion. If you are working on an inside path place a second alignment stick next to the target line stick angled toward the impact point along the path that you want the club head to follow into the ball. Rehearse in slow motion the club head approaching the bag right down that perfect path. See it and try to feel it as much as you can — let that sight and those feelings burn into your subconscious mind. Make some motion full swings (the slower the better).

Once you are thoroughly bored with the with the slow motion swings make some half swings from just the delivery position. Put some vigor into them. Make the bag pop loud. See the club head approach the bag down the line of your club path indicator. Feel the club face align perfectly to make that perfectly flush pop of the bag. Check your low point by taking a look at your shaft lean in the mirror. Check in the mirror your impact position. Does it match up with your own conception of your perfect impact? With me personally I try to get my impact to match up with the image on page 103 of Five Lessons of Hogan at impact. His right hand is a little more on top of the grip than mine, his feet are wider apart and he has more secondary axis tilt, but that's okay. I'm working on engraining my perfect impact position, not his. I believe that this type of "deep practice" is the fastest and surest way to improve your skill development. I also believe that is more important that beating hundreds or thousands of range balls. I know; this "deep practice" is incredibly boring. I wish I could force myself to go through it every day before I go out to play or practice. It is hard work, but I also know that it is the most effective tool for speeding up the process of ingraining of the skills you need to improve your golf shots.

# 16

# SWING THOUGHTS – WHAT THEY REALLY ARE – AND HOW TO REBUILD YOUR OWN GOLF SWING USING THEM

I believe swing thoughts are simply the thoughts, images, and visualizations that our conscious minds feed our our subconscious minds just before or shortly after we move the club head back. They instruct our subconscious mind on how to perform the task of hitting the ball. They can be simple (i.e., a visual image of the ball being compressed against the face of the club or the right elbow bending at a forty-five degree angle). Or they may be complicated with more than one part (i.e., the club head moving slowly back, pausing at the top, dropping down softly in transition, and then accelerating through to a full finish). I believe swing thoughts have used as long as golf has been played and will continue to be used as long as the game continues. Are swings thoughts necessary? I think to some degree yes, but as your skills develop more and more you can move from more concrete thoughts such as allowing your left shoulder to move under your chin to simply visual images like seeing a visual track of the ball fading into the target and holding that image while your subconscious takes over and carries you through your set-up and execution of the shot — sort of like watching yourself play golf. But I believe that in the early stage of creating your own golf swing fundamentals the more concrete swing thoughts will be essential. Without some direction there can be no learning.

Will concrete swing thoughts always be necessary? I don't think so. It has been reported that someone once asked Sam Snead what he thought about when he hit a golf ball. Sam looked perplexed, thought about it for a while, and then finally replied, "Nothing." I believe Sam had reached a point with his golf swing that he had lost the need for concrete "swing thoughts." He was playing golf in a state of grace. I believe other great players with strong powers of visualization also lose the need for concrete swing thoughts. I can't know, but I imagine that Jack Nicklaus reached the point where he just stood over the shot, visualized the ball flying to the target (or as he said, "Went to the movies") until he was comfortable with his visualization and then just let it happen. I think great players may sometimes become dissatisfied with their ball-striking and revert back into more concrete swing thoughts for an answer. That's just human nature. But I think they all play their best golf when they no longer need concrete swing thoughts. They play by instinct – they just visualize and go.

I think we can all reach this level of playing golf instinctively and will play our best golf when we do. However, I think we all need first to engrain a workable motor program into our subconscious. I believe that we do this through experimentation with swing thoughts and the great players used a lot of experimentation with a great variety of swing thoughts – that's simply the way the most learning takes place.

The remainder of this chapter contains a long list of swings thoughts I have come across over many years. Some are famous, some not at all. There's nothing magical about any of them. They are just thoughts that seemed to help somebody, at some time, with their ball-striking. They are worth experimenting with. Not for a week or a month, sometimes just four or five balls so that your subconscious can adjust to a new thought. If it works, good — wear it out. If it doesn't, put it aside and move on.

Before beginning the list, I will note a couple of other things about swing thoughts. Not all of them will be helpful to you. Don't get discouraged. Just put that one aside and try another. None of them will work for you forever. They all wear out, most of them quickly. Sometimes at different times in the development of your swing a thought that didn't work before, didn't even make sense before, now works. I suggest keeping a notebook of swing thoughts (what seems to work and what doesn't). When you try a particular swing thought make sure and take it to "the extreme." Sometimes exaggeration is the only way to make a change in a motor pattern. Do not be afraid to innovate. I find my most helpful swing thoughts have always been the ones I have come up on my own. Enjoy the process of building your golf swing through experimentation with swing thoughts.

<u>The Swing Thoughts</u>:

- 1) <u>Punch the dummy</u>.

While you are in your golf posture, imagine an approximate three-foot "dummy" standing on the target line just outside your forward hip. His face is just below your hip level. Draw your right fist back to just below your right shoulder. You are going to smack the dummy in the face as hard as you can with your right fist. When you do so feel the muscles of your entire body involved in the strike – the feet, legs, torso, back, arms, everything. Drive the dummy's head up through impact, up over the target line. Do this in front of a mirror, face on. Take a look. You might be in a pretty "ideal" impact position (hips forty-five degrees open; shoulders thirty). Here's an option — instead of punching the dummy, slap him with your open palm as hard as you can.

- 2) Drive the grip end of the the club in to the dummy's mouth.

Same as above except the butt of the lead palm goes to the dummy's mouth. In many ways, just the opposite of swing thought # 1. I don't agree with it but it has been suggested by Johnny Miller that dragging the handle in this way is a good idea.

- 3) The lead hand back hand slap of the dummy.

You are going to arch your lead hand under at address, or just as you start into the backswing, keep it that way at the top (visualize Dustin Johnson's arched left wrist), then slap the hell out of the dummy's face with the back of the lead wrist which is as arched as you can keep it (visualize Hogan's left wrist impact position). Someone please explain to me – why if you wanted an arched left wrist at impact, would you ever let it be cupped at the top? Wouldn't Dustin Johnson's method make more sense? You may recognize this arched wrist idea in many other modern swings such Jordan Spieth, John Rahm and Graham McDowell. Try arching the wrist as early as you can . You could even preset it at address, keep the arch at the top, then sling it right through the delivery position and on through impact. Or try the same thing but allow the arched wrist to slap release fully right at impact (the wrist feels like it goes from arched to flat to cupped in a flash burst of speed in what I would term a "release").

- 4) Skipping the stone across the pond.

(Similar to Mr. Hogan demonstrating a sidearm throw by an infielder and throwing an old two-handed basketball pass). These images may work well for those who follow Mr. Hogan's sequential downswing release ideas (from the ground up – feet then legs, then hips, then shoulders, then arms, then hands) or those who insist that the lower body must lead the upper body on the downswing. For the overwhelming majority of people they don't actually have to think about "sequencing" anything - it happens as it should naturally.

Experiment with numerous sidearm to a target throwing motions and use the ones that work best for you.

- 5) Stand still and swing your arms hard past the body.

Often works well for players who don't believe that the downswing has to be started by the lower body; that it is better dominated by the arms. It also can help those who overuse their legs. It might be an excellent swing thought for anyone considering attempting to be a pure roll squarer of the club face.

- 6) Crack it like a whip.

Remember how a whip achieves its greatest speed at the tip. The grip end moves fast then stops as the head catches up at just the right moment (right at the ball in a golf shot). Try stopping the grip end just before impact and "snapping" the head past it. Snapping a towel in a locker room is a similar swing thought.

- 7) Clothes line visual.

Imagine a sheet hanging from a clothes line. Imagine standing perpendicular to the sheet and swinging the club head into it. You want to feel what it would be like to get the club head to the sheet just before your hands get there. Yes, I know, it sounds like "flipping". Give it a try anyway. You might find a few miles per hour of club head speed. Compliments of Mike Dunaway and Tom Duke. Mike Austin, who it is said hit a drive of over 500 yards in a senior pro event at the age of sixty-four, suggested a similar image. An old Scottish pro taught him to stand next to a muddy mound hip high to his left and drive the head of the club into the mound without getting his shirt sleeve dirty. It is a very powerful image. If that's "flipping" maybe more of us should flip it. Two variations to experiment with are:

- (a) Drive the club face into the mound or;

- (b) Drive the toe of the club into the mound [I personally dislike this second option because it requires, in my opinion, early over-rotation of the forearms, but its your golf swing].

- 8) Hit it over a fifty foot tree.

Visualize a fifty foot tree that you have to hit it over. Visualize the setup and swing changes that have to take place to get it up high enough and quickly enough. Ball position forward, a little more secondary spine tilt, higher launch angle, more of a "brush" or a "pick" than a deep divot and less shaft lean at impact.

- 9) Hit a 200 yard punch shot with your seven-iron that never gets more than twenty feet high.

Yes, I know, I can't either. But if you had to, how would you try to do it. Maybe move the ball a little back, but hands well, well ahead at impact with a low finish. I don't know, maybe Jamie Sadlowski could do it. How might he do it?

- 10) Left shoulder under chin, right shoulder under chin.

This is a nice easy swing thought that sometimes helps improve tempo and balance.

- 11) Left shoulder over right knee at the top.

An old one that helps ensure plenty of weight gets right on the backswing.

- 12) 80 – 20, 20 – 80.

This is one I have used occasionally based on what the weight scales show for tour players. Imagine you are standing at address on two scales, weight balanced 50-50. As you swing to the top you move to 80% right – 20% left, as you reach impact you are 20% right – 80% left, at the finish you are 5% right - 95% left.

- 13) Face the ball at impact.

This one is courtesy of Moe Norman. I know that the hips of tour players are normally approximately forty percent open at impact (but some as little as twenty). However, the feel is what's important. I think that most people using this as a swing thought will find that they are actually open at impact, even when using this thought (I know I am). This one can be helpful for those who might think that they overuse their lower bodies.

- 14) Return to the address position at impact.

This is courtesy of Sam Snead. Obviously it is similar to #13. This might be the perfect swing thought for anyone who wisher to a pure roll squarer.

- 15) Hum a Tune.

These swing thoughts go back for a long time in the history of golf instruction. Sam Snead said he liked to hum a waltz. Instructors have long recognized the benefits of good tempo whether quicker (Nick Price) or slower (Sam Snead). I believe you should experiment with different strategies here. You might say to yourself, "one" on the backswing, "and" at the top and "two" at impact. Or a better tempo for you might be "one" going back and then "two" coming through (without the "and"), more like a Nick Price. One of my favorites was suggested by a man named Kjell Enhager in an obscure book titled "Quantum Golf: The Path to Golf". He suggested repeating to yourself the word "super" on your backswing and "fluid" on the downswing while envisioning something very fluid, such as a wet bar of soap sliding through your hands. I think the best thing about these verbal tempo thoughts is that they can take your mind off of any unnecessary mechanical thoughts.

- 16) Just think Oily.

Again, this one is courtesy of Sam Snead. There are hundreds of really simple swing thoughts that work in this same way. "Slow back," "Pause at the top," and "Slow down" are examples.

- 17) Hip bump or knee bump.

If you notice a problem with tending to hang back on the right side through impact, try feeling yourself start down with a slight bump of the hip toward the target (also experiment with both the hip bumping more towards right field or left field). Try the same things with a knee bump instead.

- 18) Hit the ball with your back still facing the target.

If you have struggled with an over-the-top issue, this one can be of help. You may be surprised at how closed you feel you can keep your shoulders and not start the ball way right. Often this one can be really exaggerated for confirmed over-the-toppers.

- 19) The Giant Circle.

Imagine the club head is as far away from your spine as you can get it at address. Now just make the biggest circle you can with the club head. Keep your arms soft back and through. Don't consciously cock your wrists. As long as your arms are soft, your wrists will cock naturally. Just make the biggest circle you can, both back and through. You might want to experiment with this one first if you believe you have issues with width.

- 20) The club face always faces the ball swing.

Imagine that at the shaft parallel position going back the club face still faces the ball (in other words, the face hasn't opened at all). At the top the face still hasn't opened at all (it will be in what golf instructors would call a shut position). Halfway down the club face again faces the ball. Envision the face slamming down on the ball with that "shut" face. Think that ball is going to go left every time? I did, but it didn't, as long as I don't have the face too closed at address. It might surprise you. This swing thought led to the technique I described in Lag and Economical Golf Swing, just another one of the infinite number of workable methods. This swing taught me something I think is important about the golf swing. It's okay to open the face of the club going back, but if you do you will have to close it back coming through. It might be easier just to leave the club face alone.

- 21) The Gatepost Swing.

This one is courtesy of J. H. Hensby. Visualize that your body is a gate. Your left foot, knee, hip and shoulder are the post. In your swing your torso just opens and closes around the post. It might be a good starting point for those who don't see the need for a weight shift in the golf swing (i.e., stack and tilt).

- 22) Hogan's pane of glass.

Feel yourself standing at address with Mr. Hogan's pane of glass on your shoulders. Swing back without breaking the glass.

On the way down, feel the plane slightly tip so that it points slightly to the right of the target line. This one is an obvious classic for feeling an inside path through the ball.

- 23) The Vertical Drop.

As the first move down, feel the club head drop softy behind you. Even feel like the club head drops a lot, even below the level of your hands. (Courtesy of Moe Norman – try it with his horizontal tug). Again, this one may help flatten your downswing path (but simply relaxing your arms as your body turns and faces the target may work even better).

- 24) The Big Swoosh.

This one is a very simple audio as well as kinesthetic feel thought. We all know that if you make a hard practice swing, the club head makes a loud swoosh sound. With some experimentation you will realize that it easy to make the sound louder without much or any thought about technique. You just swing harder – for most people, it's not any great mystery. For me, if I want to hit a driver just a little further, I just visualize making that club head swoosh as loud and for as long as I can. I don't know how it happens but I believe faster body rotation. I allow my subconscious to produce the swoosh sound. You will notice when you are actually hitting a ball that it is hard to hear the swoosh sound (I think it's because the louder sound of the crack of the club hitting the ball kind of buries the swoosh sound). I find it helpful to make practice swings focusing on the auditory swoosh. If you are interested in using the "swoosh" to increase your club head speed a little, I would recommend getting a very useful training instrument, a swing speed radar which will be addressed in Chapter 17 on the issue of increasing swing speed. I use it to experiment with my "release point". For instance, I measure some swings where I consciously try to make the swoosh as loud as I can as early as I can, or as late as I can. Or at all different points in between. Or to make the swoosh noise last as long as I can. You will quickly find what creates the most club head speed for you. Then recall that sensation when you hit a ball. Another similar thought is to make use of one of speed stick trainers that are commercially available, the ones that make a snapping noise at impact. Experiment with one of those, teaching yourself to make that thing snap as loud as you can. Then, when you hit a shot, just try to recall what it feels like to snap that stick as loud as you can.

- 25) Shoulders level through impact.

If you feel like you are making "pork chop" divots with your irons rather than "bacon strips" like Moe Norman this simple thought can work wonders.

- 26) Hit down on your irons with a four-inch forward swing bottom.

This is almost universally accepted as a fundamental of the golf swing (see e.g., Bobby Clampett's The Impact Zone: Mastering Golf's Moment of Truth), but not quite. You may want to consider and even experiment with what I consider a creative, amazing and even revolutionary alternative: hit up on everything, even your irons. Count Yogi, who was renowned as a trick shot artist, claimed he hit up on every club, even his irons and taught all of his students to do so. In fact, he ridiculed the standard golf instructions to hit down on the ball. (see,e.g., Count Yogi's Revolutionary Golf Made Easy and Five Simple Steps to Perfect Golf). Before you dismiss the Count's theories entirely, recall that some of golf's best ball-strikers have been it's biggest innovators who were unwilling to accept the platitudes of the "experts."

- 27) Just collect the ball.

Just forget the ball is there completely. You are just going to swing up to a full, flowing, relaxed top of the swing then back through to a full, flowing, relaxed finish. There is no hit at the ball — the club head just flows through the ball on its way. You may find the fully relaxed muscles here to be a surprising source of effortless power.

- 28) Some "outside the box" swing thoughts from J.H.

For a large catalogue of innovative swing thoughts you might want to consider visiting the YouTube site of J. H. Hensby, a creative and open-minded Australian golf instructor. You will find his interesting ideas and videos under 1atomicgolf.

Finally, here are my own ideas on what are the best and the worst swing thoughts. But remember, my opinions are colored by the fifty year journey I have been on through the the bewildering maze of commercial golf instruction. It has left me with the firm conviction that my best golf swing lies within the right side of my brain, not the left — I am not able to consciously "think" my way into a good golf swing, except with respect to understanding the trackman data the best I can. I believe that I have finally "grown up" and become a feel player.

I believe that the best swing thoughts are the ones that we do instinctively with the right sides of our brains — absolutely without left brain interference. Here are some of my personal favorites from many, many sources: (1) throwing a club down the fairway (underhand, overhand, or sidearm - throw it further for more power); (2) the old skipping the stone (really whip it for more power); (3) bowling (pretend it's a light ball and you're going to lob it underhand so it lands half way down the lane); (4) those basketball and infielder throws like Hogan demonstrates in Five Lessons ( But don't get all balled up in "perfect " body positions, planes, angles, alignments, "releases," etc. — just throw the damned thing like a normal human being!); (5) the grass whip idea from "Wild" Bill Mehlhorn (who Hogan said was the best he had ever seen from tee to green); (6) Henry Cotton's smacking the tire (and, in my opinion, the even better modern equivalent, the impact bag); (7) the womans' underhand fast pitch softball throw (a very powerful athletic motion similar to the longest hitters of the golf ball); and (8) the left hand frisbee throw (as far as you can). I like to mimic these motions inside, just throwing a golf ball into a net. I believe it helps to actually perform these actions in front of a mirror whenever you can. You might find something amazing — you may see body actions in the mirror that looks at least something like that of the great players of the game. You don't have to "think your way into perfect positions"; they will occur automatically every time when you get the right athletic swing thought.

I believe that when we use these natural athletic swing thoughts the they are best combined with the following realization. In an athletic (as opposed to contrived) or any powerful athletic motion the arms should never be consciously "placed" or directed. They are simply slung. Think of the outfielder throwing to home plate. He uses his arm as a whip, with no tension. He doesn't think about where to place it on his "backswing" or the angle of his wrist or elbow or whether it's on plane. He just swings it back and it goes to the perfect place for him — and not sometimes, not maybe, but every time! He doesn't control how or when the throwing wrist and elbow bend or cock. Those just occur in response to the weight of the moving ball.

And, I think the same thing should applies to our golf swings. I've found that if I get in my own grip and set-up, just leave my completely relaxed arms alone and heave them to the top with my pivot motion, they go to the same spot every time, and that is the perfect spot for me. To create a little extra swing speed the "pivot heave" is made a little more forcefully and the backswing is just becomes a little longer, but naturally, not intentionally.

Further, as long as I keep the arms fully relaxed, the weight of the club head in motion seems to "cock" the wrists and trail elbow at the right time and without any conscious thought — just like with the outfielder throwing to home plate. Please get in front of a mirror and see how that works for you. You might find you want to consider giving up conscious control of your backswing "positions" too.

I believe that the worst swing thoughts are those where you attempt to manipulate, control, or place your arms (and hands) throughout the swing. I'm sorry if you don't agree, but it is simply unnatural. You are certainly free to experiment with something like David Leadbetter's The A Swing theory if you choose. There is certainly nothing wrong with the club moving back on a "plane" above the one that it takes on the way down. But, if you are concerned about getting your downswing plane under your backswing plane, or "flattening the shaft", or "dropping the club into the slot" or any of the "ideal" positions that instructors try to move you in to, you might want to think about this. Lee Trevino famously lined up well left of his target line. He has said that this allowed his arms to move naturally outside going back. Try it for yourself in front of a mirror. Set up open like Trevino and just let your arms swing naturally back outside. Then watch what happens from the top of the swing if you leave your arms alone (just like ropes) and just turn your torso and face the target. What happens? The club will magically (it seems) drop into a clearly flatter plane, the club head drops more behind you and your hands drop into what could be described as a perfect delivery position or the perfect "slot." I don't know for sure, but I doubt seriously if Trevino ever worried about flattening his plane or dropping the club into the slot. It's just a natural response. I also seriously doubt that he ever practiced his "transition move" in front of mirror with two pages of intricate detail like is advised for students of the "A" swing. In my opinion, that type of left-brained over-think about how to position your body parts throughout the swing is the most likely type to produce an overwhelming case of "paralysis by analysis."

Finally, I have one last piece of advice in searching out swing thoughts and swing conceptions. You do not have to experiment with every new swing theory that is developed — there are an apparent infinite number of them and they will keep coming as long as golf is played. I was guilty of the practice of over-experimentation for many, many years and blindly trusting the reliability of what I know now to be very questionable sources. You can overload your subconscious mind with too much conflicting information. I believe I did. If I had to do it over again I believe that I would have been much better off in developing an athletic, powerful golf swing and honing the ability to strike the ball right out of the center of the sweet spot of the club face if I had chose a tried and true method or conception of the golf swing such as Mehlhorn's grass whip or Cotton's tire. I believe if I had trusted the method and stayed with it, I would have reached my own true potential as a ball-striker, whatever that was. I wouldn't have had to try to retrain my subconscious mind every time somebody wrote a new golf book or came up with a theory about how we could "scientifically" create the perfect golf swing. Don't make the same mistakes I did. Once you nail down your best grip and set-up fundamentals for yourself and combine them with workable impact dynamics based on the trackman information you are well on your way. Find or create swing thoughts or conceptions that give them the best results and the days of searching for a new golf swing may be over. Then you can spend your practice time on skill development. Once you've found you own swing fundamentals please stick with them and just enjoy golf.

# 17

# HOW TO JUMP YOUR CLUB HEAD SPEED TEN PERCENT IN THIRTY DAYS

You may have heard that the strongest correlation between golf handicap and various golf skills is in club head speed. In other words, if you are a middle-aged male with a driver club head speed of ninety miles per hour it is likely that you can significantly lower your handicap by increasing your driver club head speed to one hundred miles per hour (There is an assumption in here that you can maintain the quality of the strike and thereby make a corresponding jump in the number that really matters, ball speed). I use the figure of ten percent because that amount was reasonably easy for me to obtain and seems to be within the reach of almost everyone I have helped with speed.

I have come up with a simple two-part program which I believe can help anyone. The only exception would be strong, athletic players that are already maxing out their swing speed. Generally, they don't need the help.

The first part involves a swing speed drill which involves the training of fast twitch muscles by over-speed training. The second part involves combining that training with a swing thought a tour player gave me in the seventies (based on a teaching thought from Jimmy Ballard). Recently there has been a lot of talk in golf instruction about over-speed training. In my opinion, the reason is quite simply because it works. It does require some work and patience but not an excessive amount. You may have seen the Speed Stick device or the various weighted shafts used for the speed training. I wrote a short book about my own speed training several years ago titled Increase Your Swing Speed Now. I have continued to experiment with it since and have refined its ideas as follows. You will need some tools:

- 1 - An over-speed device (something with a golf grip and golf shaft that you can swing faster than your driver – my opinion – optimally about twenty miles per hour faster) (any of the commercially sold products will work – or my favorite is to drill holes in three old two-piece golf balls and epoxy them on to the end of an old driver shaft).
- 2 - A measurement device – one that can give you relatively consistent swing speeds both when actually hitting a ball and just making a practice swing. It doesn't have to match the Trackman numbers on swing speed. It only matters that you can track your progress on the same device. I recommend the Swing Speed Radar which goes for around $100.
- 3 - A small notebook or other record keeping journal.
- A suggested simple speed training program.

Day one – After you are warmed up, hit ten balls with your driver while measuring swing speed. Record the average and high speeds, then take your over-speed device and swing it ten times measuring the swing speed each time. Make each swing as hard as you can (sorry, but significantly increasing swing speed will not occur if you are swinging "easy"). Try to make each swing faster than the one before. Get some rhythm going between each swing — that usual helps keep the numbers going up. Make the "swoosh" as loud as you can make it. Experiment with what works best for you to jump the swing speed. Softening the arms and grip works for a lot of people. Even actually trying to throw or "cast" the club as hard as you can works for a lot of people. Whatever works for you. Don't worry about casting the club. Just make that thing "swoosh" as loud as you can and keep getting that number to jump.

After 10 swings you should be slightly winded. Stop and rest two minutes.

Do another set of ten the same way, using whatever swing thoughts or feelings it takes to get those numbers to jump and the device to swoosh as loud as you can. Experiment more with what makes the numbers jump. Try making a bigger shoulder turn alone and with making a bigger hip turn to enable that bigger shoulder turn. For some people, even trying to make the club swoosh as early as possible will make the numbers jump. Figure it out for yourself or use ideas you get or you have heard from other players or instructors. Stop and rest for another two minutes. Keep doing sets until your average and high numbers aren't going up any more. I can't tell you how many that will be. It might be two, it might be ten. But as long as your numbers keep going up, keep doing the sets. You are breaking barriers. Record your high practice swing number for the day and average number for the practice swings (you don't have to be precise — just something to use for you next training session). When your numbers stop going up your speed training is done for the day.

Day two — Skip at least one day before your next training session. You are taxing fast twitch muscles and they need longer for recovery. On rest days, you can play or practice, just don't do the speed training. On this day there is no need to hit balls with your driver and record the club head speed with actual shots. I suggest you not do that for the full thirty day period. Your goal for the second drill day is to exceed the practice swing numbers for the first day, particularly the high number. Keep doing the ten reps, rest cycle until your numbers aren't going up any more, then stop and record. Keep doing these drills every other day for a month. Each drill day the goal is to keep those numbers going up. If you reach a point where numbers aren't going up anymore, then take an extra rest day – you likely need more recovery time. Some days you will likely experience big jumps in speed. Take advantage of these days and get as much as you can out of them. I believe that a lot of neurological training is going on then.

Followup days — At the end of thirty days hit and measure the club head speed of ten balls with the driver using the swing thoughts that produced your highest swing speeds with the over-speed device. If you are like me, you are likely to find an approximate ten percent increase with your highest and average swing speeds with the real driver from day one. It's funny, but that ten percent jump relative to their starting numbers seems to be about the same for everyone who has gone through the drills. Make sure that on day one and day thirty the outside temperatures are comparable. No matter how warmed up we are almost all of us are able to generate significantly more club speed on a hot day than a cold one. After the thirty days are over if you keep doing the drills your numbers may continue to rise, but in my experience, it will not be nearly at the same rate. I continued with this speed training for seven months and at the end of that time I had gained another seven percent but much of that I attribute to an equipment change (lighter and longer driver shaft). In my opinion, the measurement, record keeping and goal setting are the most important part of the over-speed training. Without keeping track of your gains, it is very easy to lose interest in doing the drills and very hard to keep your effort at one hundred percent. I will note also that I stopped doing the drills after seven months and my club head speed over several years dropped back down almost to where I had originally started from. I don't believe it's something where you can "rest on your laurels" and keep the increases without continued work.

- A Simple Specific Flexibility Plan.

In the seventies I took lessons from an instructor in San Antonio named Jim Barker. He had been a tour player and a disciple of the hottest swing instructor at that time, Jimmy Ballard. In the year that I took the lessons, Ballard's ideas replaced Five Lessons as my golf instruction bible. The title of his book was How to Perfect Your Golf Swing: Using 'Connection' and the Seven Common Denominators. I was playing and practicing daily and it didn't take long until I had ingrained a pretty good version of Ballard's fundamentals. There wasn't much left to work on. I hit the ball well enough – I just didn't hit it as far as I thought I should. So, for the last six months that I worked with Jim, the only thing we worked on was figuring out how I could hit it a little further. He had a concept of "getting deep" — I assume he got it from Ballard. It wasn't the concept that instructors today are referring to when they talk about "deepness" – getting the club deep behind the right shoulder, or away from the target line. Rather, he meant taking the tip of the left shoulder and putting it way behind the ball (or as far as possible away from the target) at the top of the swing. The deeper behind the ball you got, the harder you could hit it, and for me it worked a little, but not enough to suit me. It was difficult for me to get really "deep," I think because I am stocky with broad shoulders. Eventually somebody came out with a new golf technique and I moved on. I forgot about "getting deep" for many years.

Then about two years ago, I thought about how some relatively smaller players could hit it a long way. The examples are everywhere on the pro tours (i.e., Rory Mcilroy; Rickie Fowler; and the smaller ladies on the LPGA tour). All of these players get really deep – the tip of their left shoulders gets a foot or more behind the ball at the top. The most extreme example is the relatively slight long drive hitter, Jamie Sadlowski. I don't think it's a coincidence that he gets his left shoulder deeper than any other player I could find video of. And it is irrespective of technique. I couldn't find anybody that got the left shoulder extremely deep that didn't hit it extremely long. And the opposite is also true. Think of older or inflexible golfers with low club head speed — no shoulder depth. Some of them don't even get the left shoulder tip behind the ball at all. They are never long. For virtually everyone I believe that it is a flexibility issue, specifically flexibility in the back and shoulder areas as well as in the hip area to some extent (consider John Daly's hip turn). If you suffer from a lack of club head speed, as most of us do, one of the first places to look is left shoulder depth. I don't believe it is a golf swing fundamental. As I said before, I don't believe that there are any golf swing fundamentals. I would note that there are even tour quality ball-strikers with very little left shoulder depth (see i.e., Rod Pampling and other Gary Edwin students), but not many. You might call it a quasi-fundamental (something that is helpful for most people most of the time). I started searching for a way to get more depth in my backswing. Because of body type and inherent lack of flexibility "getting deep" for me will never be easy. The traditional ideas of getting my left shoulder over my right knee or turning my left shoulder under my chin were not particularly helpful. I just wasn't flexible enough.

So I started working on my flexibility. Not overall flexibility, but specific flexibility that might increase my speed – in the shoulders, shoulders joints, back and hips. I have realized for several years that as I age, daily exercise is a requirement for continued good health. So I do yoga. Now when I do my daily yoga I go through poses that I have come up with for myself to increase my flexibility in the shoulder and back areas. I won't describe all of them (one of them is standing up in golf posture and using my right hand to pull my left shoulder as far as I can behind the ball) because I think the best drills or exercises are the ones you come up with yourself. Take a look at some video of your swing and see what your own flexibility restrictions are in the shoulder area. You can come up with your own yoga poses or stretching exercises. I believe that you are the expert on your own flexibility issues and with a little common sense and a little borrowing from the "fitness experts" who are now flooding into golf instruction on the internet you can develop your own best fitness plan to address your unique flexibility issues. Since I have begun adding the shoulder flexibility poses, I have added a little more club head speed (and ball speed). I can't tell you how much of the increase is because of the over-speed training and how much is due to the flexibility training because I do them both.

My current program is to do the over-speed training one day and then the specific yoga flexibility poses on the rest day. I suggest that you come up with a similar two-part system for yourself. In my experience, you can come up yourself with the program that works best for you. Be creative like Gary Player was when he realized that he didn't hit it far enough to win at Augusta. But I don't think your program needs to be as extensive as his apparently is. I believe that significant gains can be made in twenty minutes a day or less (combining both the over-speed and specific flexibility training).

# CHAPTER 18

## HOW TO MIRACULOUSLY TRANSFORM YOUR SHORT GAME IN A WEEK BY ABANDONING ALL STANDARD GOLF INSTRUCTION

If you read this book and decide to try some of its ideas I suggest you experiment with the ideas in this chapter first. Why? There are two reasons for that. First, in my experience, it is in the short game that insistence on correct technique can be the most damaging. Freeing your mind of these techniques can have the most impact on improving your results immediately. I am talking five minutes, not five months. Second, getting some immediate, really positive feedback may help you to trust some of my ideas. I think that is important, especially with regard to whether the ideas (I refuse to call them instruction) will take hold or whether you will move on to the next golf swing theory. Looking back over fifty years of golf swing lessons, instruction books, tapes and videos, golf magazines, YouTube videos, etc., I have come to the unfortunate realization that most of the purveyors of this instruction are at least partially, and in some cases, completely misguided. With regard to short game instruction I believe we have all been the most misled, sometimes horribly. So a healthy mistrust of any golf instruction is quite justified.

But please try the following drill and maybe I can gain a little of your trust. Take your wedge, whichever you are most comfortable with, to the putting green. Find any area of fringe where the grass is very short, like the actual green if it wasn't mowed for a day or two. Drop a ball and set up to it as you normally do (or however you would like to) with the only stipulation that the shaft be either vertical or with the hands slightly, but only slightly, in front of the ball. If you get your hands too far forward or too far back, you may not be able to accomplish the drill. Set up the sweet spot of the club face directly behind the center of the ball.

Now for the drill: brush the club head back and through. Your only thought is to not make a divot, just lightly brush the grass with the sole of the club and bounce the ball off the sweet spot of the club face. Hit a couple of soft chips this way. Forget all fundamentals – it does not matter if you do it with your hands, your wrists or your shoulders, or whether your body is open, square or closed – don't worry about flipping – just do whatever feels good to you. Soften your hands if you like so that you can easily feel the weight of the club head. Just bounce the ball off the sweet spot without marking the ground. You can actually do this on a green, but I don't suggest it. At first you may blade a few. If you do, just brush a little deeper, without taking any divot and bounce that ball off the sweet spot. Keep repeating it until your subconscious has learned to achieve crisp contact every time. It might take one minute, it might take thirty minutes (depending on how highly developed your hand-eye coordination is). Do it until the divots and/or thin shots have gone away and you are brushing the grass and striking it solid every time. Now, place three coins down at five, ten and fifteen steps (or other common chipping distance). Chip using your new brush-bounce system to the alternative targets until your subconscious is producing consistent playable shots each time.

Once you can consistently bounce the ball off the sweet spot to various targets, experiment with spinning the ball left or right the same stroke – just open or close the face a little. Experiment with trajectory some – shaft vertical for higher and softer; a little bit of forward lean to hit it lower with a little backspin. This opening or closing the face and shaft angle is about the only technique you need to consciously think about, and then only until you have ingrained it in your subconscious. Just let your subconscious mind figure out how to brush the grass at the right height while bouncing the ball off the sweet spot.

After thirty minutes of the bounce and brush drill, you should be able to hit a variety of short game shots without much, if any, conscious thought. Let the feel of the impact and visualization of the ball flight soak into the subconscious. Chipping from that one spot with one club is enough to absorb in one practice session. Next time, warm up with the same drill. Then when you feel like you are hitting nice brush-bounce chips again with your subconscious branch out to different clubs, different stances (ball below feet, above feet, uphill, downhill), different lies, different grass height. Try it for longer pitches. For each of these situations let your subconscious figure out a way to brush the sole of the club at the right through so that the ball bounces off the sweet spot of the club face. Put your mind in the sweet spot.

I had been doing the bounce-brush drills for about five practices sessions (thirty minutes each) when I realized that my short game had become transformed not just a little, but miraculously transformed. I had lost any fear of the lie, of sticking the leading edge in the ground and I had no thoughts at all of any technique. I just picked a landing spot, visualized the ball flight, let my subconscious set me up and bounce the ball off the center of the face. All that I had really done was get completely get rid of the old short game idea that we needed to put our weight left, and always "hit down" on those little shots with some forward leaning shaft. For me, it's been magical. I have no idea how I am setting up, where my weight is, if it's a shoulder swing, if I hinge my wrist, etc. I don't know and the really funny thing is I don't want to know. Now, if it is a simple shot and I visualize it correctly I expect to get up and down. I still have to practice to hone my touch and visualization skills, but I no longer worry that there is anything wrong with my "technique." I can't ask for more. It's now only about feel, judgment (such as reading the lie), club selection, creativity and visualization, all of which can be turned over to the subconscious The only "technique" left in the short game control is a bit of control of shaft lean at impact to control trajectory. I know that bouncing the ball off the sweet spot in the short game is not as important as it is in the long game. Lately I have been using a little shot sometimes where I bounce it off the fat part of the toe (there is a vertical scoring line out on the toe of my sand wedge). For me it produces a little higher, soft shot that spins to the right when it lands. Sometimes, if the lie is sketchy, I will lift the heel of the club up and bounce it off this "toe sweet spot." I don't remember ever hitting one of those and not getting an at least decent result. Should you use it? Maybe, maybe not. It worked for me – it might work for you. All I can tell you is what worked for me. I can't teach you anything about golf. All you can do is experiment. Experiment every day that you practice . If it doesn't work, file it away – it may work someday. If it does work, keep it, use it, engrain it until it doesn't work anymore, then file it away and experiment some more. You should keep experimenting to some degree as long as you play golf.

[Note – I have a friend whom I showed the brush-bounce technique to. It worked well for him. Then I saw him about a week later and he said he was having trouble hitting it solid. He said that he hit some fat when he set his weight forward. I asked him why he set his weight forward and he said, because that is what he had been taught. I suggested he not set his weight forward. He set up with his weight balanced and the problem went away. What we learned was not to mix the brush-bounce "technique" with standard golf instruction].

## CHAPTER 19

### HOW TO PUTT LIKE A TWELVE-YEAR-OLD AGAIN

The best I ever putted in my life was the period between when I was twelve and sixteen years old. Relative to the rest of my life (except this past year), I was not just better, but much, much better — ridiculously better. It seemed like I consistently made putts from everywhere. I hardly ever missed from inside five feet. On the few occasions when I did, I assumed something was wrong with the green, certainly not me. The funny thing is the kids I played with daily in the summers were the same way. We all putted better than any of the adult players at the club – even the good players that competed for the club championship. They knew not to mess with us on the putting green.

I have talked to a lot of good players about this and my experience seems to be normal. I wonder how good twelve-year-old Phil or twelve-year-old Tiger were on the greens? My guess is that they were frighteningly good.

Why is this? Why would a ball-striker reach the height of his or her skill at maybe thirty-five, but putters at maybe twelve? At first I chalked it up to the confidence of youth and, as some say, they are blissfully ignorant of how many ways there are to miss a putt. Their nerves haven't been worn out yet (Ever hear of a twelve-year-old kid with the putting yips?). Maybe it is just something about youth. But I have come up with a different theory that is consistent with my own experience, and my own observations of the best putter I have ever seen in person and the best ones I have ever heard about.

When I was twelve and first handed a putter, I was given only one instruction – how to hold it – reverse overlap rather than standard Vardon. I may have received thirty seconds of instruction. Thirty minutes of playing with it on the practice putting green and I was standing up to the ball, visualizing a path to the hole and knocking it down the path into the hole. I don't know if it was a wrist stroke, a pop stroke, a shoulder stroke, a jerky stroke, a smooth stroke, an arc stroke, or a pendulum stroke. I don't know if I was open, closed or square to the target line or if my eyes were over, inside or outside the line. I don't know if the club face was actually perfectly precisely aimed straight down the target line (I know now that is doubtful that it precisely was) or whether I actually "released the putter" (whatever that means). I don't even know if I hit it reasonably close to the sweet spot (though in all probability I guess I did). Without any other tip than how to hold it (ingrained within thirty minutes) and a little experience in reading greens I was very quickly the best putter that I would ever be.

It was not that there was no thought process when I putted. There was, but no one instructed me on it. I stood over the ball and tried as hard as I could to visualize the path the ball should take into the hole. On longer putts I looked back and forth down that path from the ball to the hole. I also knew, I suppose instinctively, that it might help to roll the ball smoothly. I just burned the vision of that path into my brain until it felt right, returned my eyes to the ball and rolled it down the path. I had no idea that rolling the ball down that line at the perfect speed was any problem at all.

I putted like this for four years and it was great. I was recently wondering how I escaped the disaster of technique fixation in my putting for four years. Then I realized that I learned technique in the full swing from Five Lessons. There is no section in Five Lessons on putting (maybe because Hogan hated putting as he made clear). It is just my opinion, but maybe the best thing Hogan did for golfers everywhere was to not write: "Five Lessons: the Modern Fundamental of Putting."

But eventually I became interested in putting technique, just like with respect to the proper technique for the full swing. Maybe when the inevitable miss occurred it was because of some flaw in my "stroke." Surely there were experts that could straighten that out too. Putting gurus such as Dave Pelz describe two basic putting methods:

- 1- Pendulum style - moving the square putter face straight back and straight through; and
- 2- Arc putting – moving the blade on a slight arc, slightly inside and opening up going back, squaring up at impact, then back inside and closing past the ball – like a mini full swing.

The "fundamentals" for both styles are slightly different. No other reasonable styles are suggested.

Whenever I hear about these two styles and that a golfer should choose between them, I invariably think of Bobby Locke. If you are under forty years old, there is a good chance you have never heard of him. However, if you had played the American professional tour in the fifties you were undoubtedly very familiar with him although he played very few times in America. This quirky South African was, in the opinion of an astounding number of those pros, the greatest putter they ever saw. According to all the accounts I have ever heard of those who actually saw him play Bobby Locke hooked everything, even his putts! The first time I heard this, I went to the practice green and tried to putt like I assumed Locke to putt. Remember, by all accounts Bobby Locke hooked his putts – not pulled but hooked. I have never even seen anyone do that even by accident. I didn't have any Bobby Locke putting fundamentals to work with. I tried to shut the face and force a sharp inside-out path. I tried to roll my hands closed through impact. I tried all types of combinations of face and path. All my attempts produced horrible results. Some went well right, some well left. I never hit anything that looked like a serviceable hooked putt. Try it sometime – you will see. Whatever Bobby Locke was doing was uniquely Bobby Locke. In my opinion, whatever Bobby Locke did to produce the magical results that he got with his putter was solely the product of his subconscious mind and couldn't be taught to anyone else. How did he learn it? I doubt that anyone taught it to him. Who would teach such a method? He probably learned it the same way virtually all unique and great styles are learned in golf — through lots of experimentations and likely lots of repetition fed into his subconscious mind.

One of the things I wonder about Bobby Locke's putting is what would have him happened if he had been forced into conventional "technique?" What if his father took a twelve-year-old Bobby to a conventional golf instructor or the Pelz Short Game Academy? Would they tell him he couldn't putt that way and stick him on a putting track that forced his path straight back and through or one of those little plastic guides and forced him to putt on an arc? My guess is they probably would. I can't think of a single golf instructor who would be honest enough to say: "Well son, I don't have any idea what you are doing, but you are a great putter. Keep knocking it in the hole. There's nothing I can teach you." And a great genius putter might have been lost. I think the greatness of Bobby Locke was the ability to teach himself his own great method, and to ignore all convention. Imagine how many times he was told, "You can't putt like that – my God, you are not even aiming at the hole." He surely recognized that his greatness came from his uniqueness.

I never saw Bobby Locke in person – I really can't say if he was the greatest putter ever, I just don't know. But I can describe the greatest putter I have ever seen (at least not under pressure).

He wasn't a tour player; he wasn't a great ball-striker (far from it). He was a guy I played maybe forty rounds with around twenty years ago. I will call him Bob. In his full swing Bob had what could only be described as an ugly golf swing. He lined up way right, had short quick backswing, and a low, very "hook" shot pattern. Like Locke, Bob hooked everything – everything, that is, except his putter – the putter he hit fiendishly straight. The first day I first played with him I thought he was probably a fourteen or so handicapper, maybe a ten if his short game was good. Then we got on the greens and he started making everything. That first time we played he made probably five putts of over twenty feet. To my way of thinking that's not just lucky — that's a virtual statistical impossibility. And he made everything inside six feet. He shot not the 84 which I reckoned he deserved based on his ball-striking, but more like 72. I thought either this is the luckiest guy on the planet, or maybe he just had the putting round of his life. I was mistaken.

Every time I played with Bob he made an inordinately high number of putts from long range and virtually all of his short ones. He could be very annoying to play with. When the inevitable miss happened he always had the same reaction: "It hit a spike mark," or "The wind came up." If the putt lipped out he always said, "They cut the hole funny."

I will describe Bob's putting style because I think it's helpful. He never took a practice stroke. He just stepped up to the ball and stared at the line for a long time, sometimes inordinately long. When he was ready he gave it a quick, sharp rap with his wrists. There was no smoothness to it at all. The best description I can give of his putting stroke is that on long putts he looked like he was trying to flip off a clod of mud that was stuck to the face of his ancient Bullseye. He said he'd had that putter since he was a kid and never saw a reason to try anything different. I guess not. On short downhill putts it was just a deft little finger stroke like a surgeon wielding a scalpel. There are some other interesting things about Bob that might help explain his attitude towards golf and, specifically putting. As best as I could tell he never practiced or even warmed up. He just played golf and I as far as I could tell, every day. He didn't take practice swings although he did stretch a little. He never talked about mechanics of either putting or the full swing. He appeared to have no interest in either. In my opinion there are a few things that made Bob such a phenomenal putter:

- 1- Total lack of faith in or interest in putting mechanics or "proper technique";
- 2- Good visualization skills and total focus on the line the ball would follow into the hole; and
- 3- Total faith in his ability (precisely his subconscious mind's) to roll it down the line and into the hole; and
- 4- A highly developed sense of touch because he relied on his fingertips to feel the club head (something that is almost non-exist among modern players who have been taught to rock their shoulders).

Basically, Bob, like Bobby Locke, putted like a twelve-year-old. Before I describe the system that I have been using for myself, there is one more thing I should mention. Remember what I mentioned about Bob staring at the line of the putt for a long time, sometimes what felt like an inordinate amount of time? I remembered another player who did the same thing. I remembered people in the seventies watching on television and saying "C'mon, when is he going to hit it?" You might remember, too. It was Jack Nicklaus.

Based on what I saw in great putters and my own putting failures I have come up with own putting rules. They are rules for me, not for you or anyone else. I suggest that you create your own, for your use. I have found that ideas I come up with on my own work best for me. I don't know why, I just know that they do. But at least consider mine. Maybe they will help you. Now I use a putter that feels good to me. I never change it.

When I putt I think about zero fundamentals — none. I have no pre-shot routine. I normally read the putt from whatever place feels comfortable, sometimes above and below, sometimes just one of those. I read the putt until I feel comfortable with my read. Sometimes I make a practice stroke. Sometimes I don't. Whatever feels good to me. When I am comfortable I stand up to the ball and put the club face behind it generally pointing the face down the target line. I don't worry at all about my "stroke." I don't even concern myself with how perfectly I have aimed the face unless it's a short putt (inside ten feet or so — then I try to be very precise with the face). I just "softly" aim it down the target line and trust my subconscious to take care of the rest. I don't get ball bound. Instead, I immediately get "line bound." I burn that line into my brain as much as I can. I trace the line from the ball to where I want it to enter the hole. If I am not comfortable with it, I trace it again, even a third time. I do it again until I am comfortable with the line. Sometimes it is one time. Sometimes it is more. I don't worry about how many times it takes to get comfortable. I just do it until I am comfortable. Then I glance back to the ball, and let my subconscious roll it down the line. I don't let my gaze linger over the ball. When I gaze back to the ball from the target line I personally don't think much at all about distance. I guess I am just turning speed over to my subconscious. I am almost always amazed at how good my subconscious is at judging speed. If the ball goes in, I pick it out of the hole and remind myself what a great putter my subconscious mind is. If it misses, I assume it hit a spike mark or the greenskeeper screwed up the hole – after all, I am the best putter in the world. With this approach, while I am maybe not the best putter in the world, I do again putt like I did when I was twelve.

If you have any continuing concerns about the possible benefits of proper "technique" in the art of putting please view the following approximately seven minute video on YouTube: "Count Yogi Palm Springs 1960 Putting Exhibition." After you've watched it ask yourself what putting technique is on display as he rolls in all of those devilish little sidehill breaking putts with all those different implements? And whether today's short game gurus with their face-balanced putters and putting tracks would have been willing to putt against the Count for money? Or if any of those gurus would be willing to put on a public "putting exhibition" to demonstrate the validity of their techniques? Or if using your fingers a bit to feel the putter head might improve your touch just a little. If you are interested in some "skill development" for your putting touch try this drill. Take one ball and the your sand wedge to the putting green and experiment for thirty minutes with putting with the sand wedge's leading edge. Just use your fingers and wrists. Observe and feel the incredible touch you develop in a short period of time without any concern about "technique."

# CHAPTER 20

## CONTROLLING SHOT LENGTH

Controlling shot length is one of golf's most critical skills. Great ball-strikers do it by instinct. Poor ball-strikers have little control of it and many don't even have a logical plan for how to do it. For many years, I didn't. I had a sort of nebulous three-quarter punch shot that I used when I was between clubs. About six months ago I saw the first small launch monitor for under $200. It provides only limited information, but ridiculously useful information if the information was reliable. It measures ball speed, club head speed and for my purposes most importantly, carry distance. I found that it measured ball speed and club head speed somewhat accurately, at least with side-by-side comparison to the much more expensive Trackman and Flight Scope units. But with respect to carry distances the readings were inconsistent at best. For me, it overestimates driver carry distance and underestimates carry distance with irons, especially with the critical wedges and short irons. It is often ten yards or more in recognizing carry distances to targets measured accurately with the highly precise range finders. I don't know what accounts for this inaccuracy. I just know that I couldn't count on the device to establish my own personal carry distances for each club.

But, my little launch monitor did prove very helpful for one purpose — helping me find my own personal way of controlling shot length. One of the first things I noticed when I first started using the unit, was that if I choked up right to the metal on my seven-iron (right index finger just on the metal) and made my normal swing, the ball flew almost exactly my full eight-iron distance (although on a lower trajectory). I played around with that concept and found that it applied very well throughout the bag. So I came up with a plan that for me is very simple and workable. Where I grip the club depends on how far below my full shot carry distance I want. I try to make it proportionate. Here is an example – my full eight-iron carry is 155 yards; seven-iron is 170 yards. Suppose I need to carry it 161. That's 2/5 of the way between 155 and 170, so I try to grip it 2/5 of the way up the grip from the metal. For me, this has worked exceptionally well. But it does have the disadvantage of almost never hitting two shots in a row on the course with your grip in the same position. And for a while it may feel very awkward choking down to the metal on a full shot. But it is a workable option.

I am not saying that you should adopt this method of distance control. Some good players use different length swings, different speed swings, or even combinations of all three. But I think you are better off finding one that works well for you and sticking with it. It is a critical skill that can only be honed through practice and experience. And you will not enhance your skill if you change your personal golf swing "fundamentals" every time another new swing theory catches the golfing public's fancy.

The skill of controlling shot length is of its most critical importance in the area of half-wedges (for me, the thirty to one hundred yard range). They are shots that every player, no matter what their playing level or handicap or how carefully they try to plan around them, will face in virtually every round of golf. Often they will face many of them and they are particularly critical to scoring.

There are a number of approaches that are suggested for these crucial partial shots. You may be familiar with the multiple wedge system combined with a clock system of varying backswing lengths suggested by Dave Pelz. I tried it and it didn't work for me. I even had the numbers written up and down the shafts of my wedges to keep it all straight. On the driving range it worked very well. But for me, when I got on the course and needed to hit real golf shots under real conditions (downhill, uphill, down wind, into the wind, high trajectory, low trajectory, more spin, less spin, hot day, cold day, lot of adrenaline, no adrenaline, etc.) it was an utter failure. It was another case of way too much information and way too much left-brained input.

My own solution for dealing with the half wedges is to try to simplify the process and turn it over to my subconscious mind as much as I can. I now only use one wedge for wedge shots in this distance range — my 56 degree sand wedge. It simplifies the whole thing for me mightily. I recognize that feel combined with good visualization is going to be my only way to get better at controlling these distances and that I will only be able to do that through practice and experience. My "grip ladder" method of controlling shot length with the other irons is only very partially useful with these shots. I recognize that while the "backswing clock" information is certainly useful, it is very, very incomplete.

Here is how I attempt to train my feel with respect to these shots. I find three reference targets on the practice range at twenty-five, fifty, and seventy-five yards as precisely as I can. There is no magic to those distances - they are just easy for me to remember. I always use the same three distances. I ignore the carry distance and don't do the "training" if it is very windy. I hit as many shots as I can trying to hone in on those precise distances. Sometimes I'll hit several in a row to the same target until I get it precisely dialed in. When I do that I'll switch to one of the other two targets. I am generally aware that on the "backswing clock" my twenty-five yard shot is going to be around seven o'clock, the fifty yard shot around eight o'clock, and the seventy-five yard shot around nine o'clock. On the course I try to use the feels of those three reference swing distances (and my full swing sand wedge distance) to estimate the right feel for the distance involved (after factoring in wind and trajectory of all of the information that goes into visualizing the right shot for the situation). I try to never think about the "backswing clock" or or any mechanical thought on the golf course. Using this simple method I'm not great at this but I'm much better than I was when I tried to mechanically think myself through the process of hitting half-wedges. The only way to improve at this skill is through continued practice and experience. There is no golf theory, method, or technique in the world that can explain to you how to hit a sixty-seven yard sand wedge to a tight pin on a rock hard green. Only judgment, visualization, feel and experience honed through repeated practice can help you there. Find of your own method of controlling shot length and stick with it.

# CHAPTER 21

## A SUGGESTED MODEL FOR YOUR NEW GOLF SWING BASED ON THE DESIGN CHARACTERISTICS OF THE PROPERLY DESIGNED CLUB AND THE REAL "ALTERNATIVE" SWING THEORY

I do not have much knowledge about the history of golf club design — how and why all the features of these "instruments" (such as length, lie, loft, weight, shape of club head, sole, relationship of club head to shaft, etc.) that we use in golf came to be as they are today. I do know that no "scientist" or group of experts ever sat down and in a vacuum analyzed how a theoretical game of "golf" might be played and came up with design characteristics that would be ideal for fourteen separate instruments that would make it most helpful and most efficient for humans to hit the shots required by such a game. Rather, I am sure that the design characteristics of the clubs that we use today came about through five hundred years of evolution of the instruments primarily through experimentation by club makers and players. Club makers were normally players and they adjusted the designs of the clubs to find what worked for them and for their customers (normally the more skilled players). Occasionally creative players and club makers made new innovations that rapidly contributed to the evolution of the instruments (i.e.,

Gene Sarazen and the sand wedge). As materials and conditions changed new innovations were made in the clubs' design characteristics and eventually we ended up with the fourteen (assuming we play by the rules) that we use today. This all would have only been of academic interest until the other day when I had a stunning and amazing (at least to me) realization about our modern golf clubs. I doubt that I am the first to come to this realization but I have never heard it expressed. I will describe how I came to this realization below.

I was working with an impact bag, a mirror and my driver. I think it is important that you use the driver to experience this because it's easiest to feel when that huge sole is soled properly on the ground. I was in my own athletic preferred (rock-skipping) set-up with my preferred grip assembly (imitating impact). The driver was completely soled a couple of inches behind the ball and to me appeared slightly open to the target line as I now believe it logically should. I suddenly had the realization that the club was perfectly "designed" to easily accomplish its intended purpose to move straight back and straight through on the arc that the club was sitting on at address. So I let the club move back on that arc. The only intent that I had was to feel the soled club be left in that properly soled position for the first few inches of the backswing. It produced the old "caddy drag" motion that older players like Bobby Jones used. Moving the club head back either inside or outside of that arc would feel awkward and unnatural — try it and I think you will notice it immediately. I found that once that starting direction was established momentum carried that club head right up to the perfect top of the swing position for me assuming I just stayed relaxed, did nothing to interfere with its motion or direct the path in any way. I had the definite sensation that the club was moving itself. Assuming I left the arms soft the wrists cocked naturally from the momentum of the heavy club head on its arc. The right arm naturally folded just as it should. As for the downswing the feeling is that the club head just reverses and comes right back that same arc that was described by that perfectly soled club at address. My grandmother had an expression, "I just gave the horse its head." I assume she just meant to let go of conscious control of the instrument (the horse), or in my case, the club head. The most interesting thing about letting go of control of the instrument is the feeling of ease, grace and fluidity that it creates. If you can disregard any thoughts of trying to consciously coil, turn, swing fast or hard, or otherwise do anything that might create tension or disturb the arc of the moving club head I think that you will find that the swings that occur once you let go of control are the most graceful, fluid and consistent you've ever made. It works with every club in the bag. The arcs are a little different with each club ( the arcs get more vertical as the clubs get shorter), but that is dialed in by the lie angle, and after dragging the sole back on it's arc for that first few inches, there is no need to worry about it further.

I believe that one of the things that you need to consider when building your own golf swing and its fundamentals is your overall conception of what the golf swing really in its essence is. Like everything else in golf (and life) multiple theories are available: a side arm throwing motion; a circle; an ellipse; a backhanded slapping motion; a circle with a lever; a multiple lever system; a turn around one axis; a two-axis system; a pivot action; a spring being wound and released; or a club head orbiting around a central point (normally somewhere around the sternum bone). Nobody really knows which of these is "right'," but I believe each player needs to find their own most useful conception to base his or her fundamentals around. I suggest you consider this one: it's the fluid motion of a club head back and through the ball on the arc described by its design characteristics (specifically the lie angle). Or, maybe less elegantly, let the club do what it was wonderfully "designed" to do. Let the club swing itself is now my favorite swing thought and and overall swing concept at the same time.

When I first realized the fluidity and grace and utter lack of muscular tension required to leave the club alone on its proper arc it reminded me of something I had heard from an old source from fifty years ago. Recall when I mentioned in the introduction to this book that when I first took up golf I chose to follow the teachings of Five Lessons rather than the outlandish ideas of an obscure trick shot artist who called himself Count Yogi. I recalled something Count Yogi had written about his golf swing being totally boneless, muscleless, effortless, perfectly balanced and perfectly graceful. So I looked up and found video of the Count hitting golf shots from when appears to be the forties, fifties and sixties. In spite of my initial aversion to his hyperbole about his talent I had to admit that his description of his own golf swing was completely accurate — it is the most elegant and graceful golf swing I have ever seen. He also appeared to swing exactly the same way with every full shot no matter what the club. I was intrigued, so I located and read copies of two of his instruction books : Revolutionary Golf Made Easy and Five Simple Steps to Perfect Golf. I won't try to summarize his theory of the golf swing but I realized that at it's core it appears to me to be based on a concept very similar to the one that I had realized: that each club should be just moved straight back on the arc prescribed that the design of the particular club (the lie angle) without any muscular tension or interference and it comes back though the ball on that same arc. But then he adds another truly revolutionary concept to his theory — every shot should be "hit up on" as the club moves back up the arc into the finish, even the irons. It is completely contrary to every golf swing theory about impact that I am familiar with. But by all accounts he was an exquisite ball-striker. He instructed his students to never hit down on any shot and never intentionally take a divot. It suggests to me that an assumption underlying this "never hit down" theory may be that each club is designed to be hit with its true loft. It also appears contrary to the idea I have heard espoused that today's irons at least are "designed" to be hit with a forward leaning shaft. And I will agree that I'm still trying to figure how to hit an iron off a tight lie without risking getting it just a little bit fat. It may be that the design of our irons now has changed so much since the Count's day that his theory of hitting up on his irons is no longer consistent with the design characteristics of the instrument (i.e., with most modern clubs the leading edge of the sole is thicker, the bounce of the sole is greater and the shaft leans a little more toward the target). It appears to me that the design characteristics encourage more of a downward strike than those of the clubs the Count may have used.

I believe that there is a very strong possibility that Count Yogi, instead of being a bizarre eccentric as he was labelled, may have been a true golfing genius. His ideas, though very short and clear are also elegant, brilliantly inspired and make more sense to me now than all the other golf instruction published in the world since 1957. If I could do it all over again I believe that day fifty years ago I would have put Mr. Hogan's book back and taken the Count's with me. Of course, now every time I missed a shot somebody would say, "You flipped it again." To which I could respond, "Yeah, but I looked good, didn't I?"

# CHAPTER 22

## SEVEN LAST TROUBLESOME QUESTIONS IN GOLF SWING "THEORY"

Over the years I have struggled with seven recurrent questions about the golf swing (mainly regarding potential swing speed) that I was never able to get reasonable answers to. I finally resolved them to my own satisfaction. I will give you my opinion on them now because there is a good chance you will have them, or variations of them, when you build your own golf swing.

- 1.- Can a player generate more club head speed by employing some degree of forearm roll through impact (what I now call a roller or a blend) or, as what I would now call a "pure body squarer "?

In the eighties, Tom Watson wrote a book where he advocated rolling the forearms over through impact, sort of "crossed swords," which I now term a roller. Many instructors seem to believe that you can significantly bump club head speed by squaring the club that way. As I've said a pure body-squarer would be more like Jordan Spieth where the the involuntary forearm rollover does not occur until significantly past impact.

Would Jordan Spieth add some club head speed by consciously utilizing some rollover? No one can say for sure but based on my own experience I would say no. I have done a lot of experimenting with launch monitors and radar devices and have been unable to realize any speed gains by any form of "rolling the forearms" through impact. None. In fact, for me personally, the swing thought that most often produces my maximum club head speed is the Mike Austin "flip" (which is actually the action that I now define as the "release" of the club). If you are distance hungry it is something you might want to experiment with but don't be surprised if your swing speed stays about the same. And my common sense tells me that a pure rotator like Spieth might lose some of his wonderful accuracy with conscious forearm rollover.

- 2- Does "weight shift" significantly add to club head speed?

Traditional golf instructors would say yes. Single-axis and double-axis options are available. I suppose the best known single-axis option would be Stack and Tilt. I would argue that the "Gary Edwin Right-Sided Swing" model fits in this category, as do a few others. Arguably they are simpler models. In my experience, I have found that I can generate a little more club head speed by allowing a weight shift, but for me surprisingly little – about two miles per hour. I have seen players who have the same swing speed with a single-axis model and a double-axis models. I have never seen anyone swing faster with a single-axis model then they could with a double-axis model. One of the Bennet and Plummer videos has some footage of tour player Troy Matteson hitting a driver while standing on two force plates. I recall one where he carried a driver over three hundred yards with ninety percent of his weight on the left side at the top of the swing. But he is a big guy and a stronger tour player. To me all this suggests that a dual axis system may have some speed gains possible, but the amount is greatly exaggerated. Again, this is an area where you need to test yourself with a Swing Speed Radar or similar device. One final thought on weight shift – perhaps weight shift may allow for a longer backswing which may be the actual reason for any speed jump.

- 3- Will a strong grip generate more swing speed than a weak grip?

This one gets back into the area of lag, or of a late release. Most golf instructors seem to believe that a stronger grip allows for the retention of lag further into the downswing (and thus arguably more club head speed). I have tested this quite a bit for myself and find I have the same club head speed for a "one-knuckle" grip or a "three-knuckle" grip. I also note that Hogan's lag retention in the period of Power Golf where he used a stronger grip and later in the fifties when he adopted a weaker grip appears pretty much the same. The swing was shorter with the "weaker" grip but the lag appears the same. Again, this is an area where I suggest testing yourself. I believe, though, that as long as the club is in the fingers of the left hand, as opposed to the palm, the relative "strength" of the grip may not be important.

- 4 - Does the lower body starting the downswing, as opposed to the upper and lower bodies starting down together, lead to any increase in swing speed?

For many, many years I believed that the lower body lead was an absolute foundation to a great golf swing. The big rubber band attached to the left hip illustration in Five Lessons strongly suggests that. Many, if not most, golf instructors will tell you that one big difference between good and poor players is that the good ones start their lower bodies down first. For me, it was not a good piece of instruction nor was starting the lower body forward while the upper body was still going back. One reason is that it is simply difficult for many people ( myself included) to do. The drill that is most often taught to those who endeavor to start the "bottom" first is the "baseball step-drill". You can find dozens of variations of it demonstrated on YouTube and I am not going to describe it here. I will say that for me while doing the drill is very easy, striking golf balls well while doing it was always very difficult, and no matter how much I tried to drill it in, I could never get it engrained as my motor pattern. My body just doesn't work that way.

Another thing I noticed when large amounts of stop action video became available on the internet was that I couldn't see the amount of lower body lead in the videos of the "great" swings that others were apparently seeing. Sometimes, I could see a very, very little. It was never what I would call significant. But what I most often saw, and still see today, is that the left knee and the left shoulder, even in Hogan's swing, appear to start back down simultaneously. Maybe I am missing something. But don't believe me. Take a look for yourself.

Even if we assume that there was a lower body lead in the swing of the great players, it was undoubtedly a small one. But did that small lead actually add anything to the swing? I am now satisfied that if it did, it was very, very little. I base my opinion on a couple of things. First, I did a lot of experimentation with the swing speed radar and found that no swing thought of firing the hips first, or driving the legs, or the rubber-band left hip connection created any club head speed increase for me. Nor did my swing speed change at all. It was simply the same. Second, you may be familiar with trick shot artists who hit shots while sitting in a chair and still keep about ninety percent of their length. I would suggest that if their chairs were taller, and their swing arcs were more normal they would be able to get much closer to one hundred percent of their normal club head speed.

There are some golf instructors who teach initiating the downswing with the arms and using your legs more like stabilizers than initiators. To me, that seems like a workable option also. Separating the lower body torso turn from the upper body torso turn on the way down did not lead to any change in club head speed for me. It might for you — again you need to experiment with it for yourself. All the "sequencing" theory and drills did for me was cause mishits. I suggest that before you decide to make "sequencing" one of your downswing fundamentals you look for some empirical evidence that it does anything to improve your club head speed or your other launch conditions. It will be tough to time. What continues to work best for me is to fire the entire torso (shoulders and hips) together in an aggressive turning motion to and past the target — Hogan's "turn and face the target" quotation. But if you find you can gain power by "sequencing" the hips and shoulders, then, "more power to you." I believe that it happens so fast that it is out of our conscious control. If you believe in a "sequencing " theory, I also suggest that if you simply visualize an analogous athletic motion like skipping the stone on pond (or take your choice of the others previously) you'll find that your subconscious mind will "sequence" all of the body components very nicely.

- 5 - Can "ground forces" be used to significantly increase club head speed?

If you have been interested in golf instruction in the last ten years, you have no doubt come across the term "ground forces." It refers to the use of the ground on the downswing as a "springboard" that the player pushes against to generate extra club head speed. You will see it in the swings of young, athletic LPGA and PGA tour players. Two good examples are Lexi Thompson and Bubba Watson. The primary characteristic of players who use these ground forces well are that at impact their lead heel will be off the ground, maybe even the whole left foot. You can also see the move in swings that go as far back as Bobby Jones and before.

I believe that you can add some swing speed with such a "jumping" move through impact. How much, I am not sure. A couple of miles per hour maybe? I am just guessing. I know that I have tried it, although not much, and it doesn't help me. It may be that I am just too old to make such a dramatic change in my gross motor pattern. But it is evident in virtually all of the swings of long drive competitors. I suggest that if it is in all of their swings, it must have some capacity to increase club head speed.

In designing your own golf swing is it something you should consider? I think if you do it naturally I would certainly not try to train it out of your swing. If you need distance, I believe it is something you should explore. Also, if you want to be a pure body squarer I believe it is something to at least experience since you will being relying so heavily on your feet and legs in your golf swing. If you are interested in "ground forces" you might want to experiment with it in this fashion. Set an impact bag up behind a low barrier to keep the bag from moving and set up the mirror so that you can check your impact position from the target viewpoint. Make some half swings from the delivery position squaring up the face with just body turn, trying to get as much of your body to face to the target at impact as you can. Slowly build up the intensity of each strike. Make the bag pop louder each time. Don't add any forearm roll, just pure body-squaring. You may find eventually that at impact virtually your entire torso is facing the mirror and your hands are just off your right hip. If you are going to be a pure body rotator I believe that is a very good thing to cultivate. If you keep increasing the speed and intensity of your body rotation you will eventually realize that your heels are coming a little off the ground at impact. And it is very likely that you will be "smashing the stuffing" out of the impact bag. I believe that this "jumping" action is not the result of anything a player can actively do with his or her feet ( there would be no way to time it). Rather, I believe it is the result of just keeping your feet well-grounded early in the downswing and a very, very aggressive torso turn. Once you've felt it with the impact bag I think the feeling will be easy to transfer to your golf swing. It will feel like you are hitting the ball with your feet.

I saw an article recently about something called parametric acceleration. I don't pretend to understand what it is other than long hitters sometimes appear to move the left shoulder up and back away from the ball through impact. In my opinion, they are describing another aspect of the ground force phenomena, i.e.; that some players can generate a little extra speed through driving with the legs and "standing up" through impact. In my own experience I have not been able to realize any speed gain by consciously driving my legs up off the ground through impact. But I have on occasion noticed that when I try to hit a driver hard (for me it feels like with my entire body) my left heel will actually rise just a little bit through impact. But it's nothing I am trying to do with my legs. I am just guessing but I doubt that Bubba Watson thinks much at all about what his legs are doing through impact. I think he is most likely thinking, "Hit it hard," or something similar. My advice is that you let your subconscious decide whether it needs to use parametric acceleration to hit it hard.

- 6 - What is the most athletic posture for golf?

As I mentioned earlier I do not like to isolate the elements of set-up from each other but it has been very helpful for me recognize the extremes that are taught and have been used successfully by great players over the last one hundred years with respect to one single aspect of posture — spine angle at address. Modern players are taught to and tend to bend much more from the hips with "their butts stuck out out behind them." I believe these positions have arisen from notions describing an athletic set-up as similar to "guarding someone in basketball" or "preparing to dive from the edge into a swimming pool" as opposed to Hogan's "sitting on the spectator stick," which produces a more vertical spine and a "tucked under butt." [I only know of one contemporary golf professional who teaches this tucked under posture, a California pro, George Gankas].

If you look back to the players preceding Hogan you see an overwhelming number of postures that resemble Hogan's spectator stick analogy (with some variation to account for for height and other body dimensions). Why is there such a difference? I can only speculate but I suggest it may be at least in part due to the conception in the literature at the time that the best way to swing a golf club was to "turn in a barrel" attributed to Percy Boomer. Ideally it would be one barrel to turn the hips and shoulders together in — not one barrel for the the lower body to remain relatively stationary in and another severely tilted barrel (up to forty degrees) for the torso to turn in. I have experimented with both the "one-barrel" and "two-barrel" systems over the years — for the most part with two-barrel systems because that is what the modern "experts" taught. As soon as I was able to free myself from conventional theory I quickly realized that any two-barrel system is a horrible choice for me. Not only does it diminish my swing speed by retarding my hip turn and consequent shoulder turn (as much as five miles per hour) but it is relatively awkward, unbalanced, and more likely lead to an arm-dominated downswing. As a wonderful bonus when I found my way into a more one-barrel posture through the rock-skipping set-up drill the lower back pain that I had been suffering with for twenty years magically vanished within a few weeks. Experiment and find which works for you, especially if you are tall. The one-barrel option can be very difficult for tall people — it is difficult to get the club down to the the ball without a lot of spine angle.

The most extreme example of what I call the two-barrel posture is a drill used in a methodology that came into vogue about ten years ago: Jim Hardy's Plane Truth for Golfers. I won't describe his swing theory other than to say he lumps all golf swings into two groups: (1) one-plane — where the arms swing on roughly the same plane as the body (as I recall, the plane of the shoulders); or (2) two-plane — where the arms swing on a plane more vertical than the the body swing plane. He then describes "fundamentals" for each of these two groups of golf swings. It sounded intriguing, so again I took the bait. I read both of his books, tried out both of his sets of fundamentals to see where I best fit in. I didn't hit the ball any better with either — in fact, I couldn't stop hooking my driver with either set of fundamentals even with my "weak" grip. I assumed that there must have something wrong with how I was applying the fundamentals. I figured I would need an expert eye. So I signed up and went to one of his two-day academies. It was expensive for me: over a thousand dollars and my wife was not amused.

Mr. Hardy wasn't there but two of his assistants were. One of them even claimed to be teaching a tour pro, although today I can't remember which one. There were about a dozen of us students. The instructors watched us hit balls for about fifteen minutes. I became sort of embarrassed when I realized that I was the only student who might even conceivably be a low handicapper. Then they divided us into two groups: the one-planers and the two-planers. One poor man who I had noticed whiffing a few shots was taken away for separate instruction as a two-planer. Apparently he was the only two-planer in the group. After he was taken away we were assured that one-plane swings were more athletic and we would need more "athletic" set-ups — in their view wider stances and significantly more bent over hips (thirty to forty-five degree spine angles). Of course, I already knew this and had mastered it from the books and dvds I'd purchased. I even knew what was coming next. A man appeared from the clubhouse carrying a large plastic trash can that the bottom had been cut out of — the one essential training tool of of the "one-plane training academy." I'm not joking. Mr. Hardy's training device had turned Percy Bloomer's wonderful "turn in a barrel" concept on its head. Now in an "athletic swing" the player wouldn't be turning his entire body in one barrel but locking a lower body barrel in place (with the wide stance) tilting the torso in a second barrel at an uncomfortable and unnatural angle above it and then twisting the upper barrel against the lower. I suggest today that this posture might not be "athletic" for any purpose other than jumping off of something, like maybe a high building. One-by-one the other students (I now call them victims) were encouraged to spread their feet wide while the trash can was placed over their torsos so they could feel how to rotate in the upper barrel with their new "proper" spine angle. I wasn't required to go through the humiliation of the barrel drill myself and was encouraged to go off and hit balls by myself — apparently, I had already demonstrated the ability to spread my feet wide, bend over at a forty degree angle and torque my upper body against my lower.

If you are wondering what benefit I got from my expensive experience at the Plane Truth Academy I can only say not much. The instructors left my "one-planer" fundamentals alone. To address my issue with hooking the driver they only offered me this tip: push down with the right palm heel pad on the base of the left thumb through impact. It worked for about three balls, then I started blocking it when I apparently pressed down on the left thumb a little too hard. I never got any consistency with the "press the thumb" tip. I never gained anything positive from either the one-plane or two-plane techniques. I did not gain any club head speed or strike the ball any more accurately. I now realize the obvious that the thumb press was just a band-aid temporary remedy, not anything to do with any one-plane fundamental or any other fundamental. It's likely it just held off a little forearm rollover to keep the club face from closing as quickly. It is also very likely, in fact overwhelmingly likely, that if I had known then what I know now about the trackman fundamentals, club face alignment at address and the path follows face phenomenon, that my driver hooking issue would have immediately resolved by the absurdly simple solution of opening the club face a little at address. With regard to Mr. Hardy"s one-plane and two-plane principles or any other body plane discussions that have been beaten to death in the literature I now believe that while they might be of some interest theoretically, the "plane" of any part or section of the body is absurdly irrelevant in terms of improving your golf swing. In my judgment, the only "plane" worth considering is the plane of the club shaft itself since it perfectly traces the arc of the moving club head.

I would like to mention one more thing about posture. One of the issues that comes up frequently with the modern golf swings which have more spine tilt at address is the difficulty of "staying in your posture." In my opinion it is purely the result of excessive spine tilt at address. I believe that if you bend too much from the waist and let your rear end stick out maintaining that posture is always going to be an issue for you. In an effort to make a powerful and accurate swing your body will naturally try to "release" that spine angle. On the other hand, if you assume a posture with more a more vertical spine at address with your buttocks under you rather than sticking out behind you will likely have no issue at all with "losing your angles." Most likely, the opposite will occur —you will gain some spine angle at impact. If you'll look at YouTube video of Hogan down-the-line at the address, the top of the swing and the impact positions you should be able to see more more spine angle at the top of the swing and impact than at address, in some videos remarkably more. You'll find the same in video of Sam Snead and virtually all of the great players prior to 1950. Apparently the issue of "coming out of your posture" didn't exist until modern instructors began to teach students that it was more athletic to bend more at the waist and let your rear end stick out.

- 7 — Can power or swing speed be increased by torquing the upper body against the lower body in the backswing and then releasing it on the downswing?

In 1997 noted golf instructor Jim McLean released a book entitled The X-Factor Swing that became an immediate sensation in golf instruction circles. The underlying premise of the book is still a staple of contemporary golf swing theory today. That premise is that the differential between the angles of a player's hip turn and shoulder turn create torque between the upper and lower body which can be used to create power. Theoretically, the differential between the two angles can even be increased in the early stages of the downswing further enhancing the release of energy through impact. Scientific measurements of the differentials between the hip and shoulder angles in some tour players were presented. The results appeared to confirm the theory — the pros with the biggest differentials hit it the furthest; those with the least differential hit it the shortest. John Daly was the poster child for the theory. He had the biggest differential measured and as most people know, he hit it the furthest.

When I first read about this X-factor theory I was overjoyed. Obviously this was an easy way to pick up the extra burst of club head speed that I was looking for. So I worked at it for several months. I kept my hips still, even resisting their inclination to turn, as I torqued my shoulders against them. On the downswing I tried to increase the torque by turning my hips back through before the upper body could get started. It all sounded good. The problem was I didn't hit it further, I actually couldn't hit is as far. I think I know now why I lost instead of gained club head speed. Retarding my natural hip turn resulted in less shoulder turn which resulted a shorter swing arc and less swing speed. Moreover, I believe the tension the torquing action creates also reduces fluidity and club head speed. I have found that for me relaxed muscles equal faster muscles. Since I first got the swing speed radar unit about ten years I have experimented with it on numerous times with a torquing X-factor swing and a relaxed "zero-torque" full swing with the biggest hip and shoulder turns I can make. For me the full zero-torque swing is always at least five miles per hour faster. I suggest that you find a radar device and experiment with both ideas yourself. However, if you decide that you need a significant amount forward spine tilt at address and to use "X-factor torque" as your primary power source be ready for the possibility of some lower back issues.

Shortly after the publication of the The X-Factor Swing another idea was published by McLean in a cover story in a issue of Golf Digest titled "The Y-Factor." I boil the Y-factor idea down to this simple concept: the deeper you can get the tip of the left shoulder behind the ball at the top, the more potential you have for creating club head speed. Of course, this is the same Jimmy Ballard idea that came to me through Jim Barker and was mentioned in Chapter 17 of the present book regarding increasing club head speed. I believe that the Y-factor idea is a wonderful idea and the easiest way to create extra club head speed as long as you don't try to combine it with the X-factor concept of torquing the upper body against the lower. I believe they are inconsistent. Here's why. To get to your full depth of the tip of the left shoulder behind the ball anatomically you have to allow the hips to fully open up. And if you allow the trail knee to straighten a little you can even get more "Y-Factor." Get up and try it — you will notice it immediately. I think that the biggest "Y-factor" you'll find is when you can remove any tension or "torque" out of you back and allow (not force) the biggest hip and shoulder turns you can. Try just making a big relaxed hip turn (the shoulders will follow) in front of a mirror. You may find it looks something like Bobby Jones and that you may also find the most "Y-factor" you've ever experienced. There is one further thing you might want to note about the X-factor/Y-factor dichotomy. The cover model for the Golf Digest Y-factor article was Vijay Sigh. If you will take a look at video of his golf swing through the years (particularly with the driver) you will see plenty of hip turn and a relaxed rather than a torqued back. The same is true for video of John Daly — his full hip turn is reminiscent of the pre-1950s players (even significant straightening of the trail leg) and a relaxed, not torqued back. I seriously doubt that either of these powerful modern swingers ever thought of torquing their upper bodies against their lowers.

I fully recognize that as of 2017 this X-factor "torquing for power" remains fully ensconced in standard golf swing instruction. I only suggest that before you make it one of you personal fundamentals you experiment with some other options and consider whether there might be a more comfortable, more powerful, more athletic and even a safer way to obtain club head speed. I will make one final observation. I believe that it is almost universally conceded that Tiger Woods was the most physically gifted athlete that we have seen in the history of professional golf. If you look at video of his golf swing throughout the years you will see the purported "athletic" posture that is now treated as standard ("guarding someone in basketball" and a straight spine) and a clear torquing of the upper body against the lower. It is as if the modern conception of the golf swing motion is of a spring (the spine) that is to be tightly wound and then unwound. Tiger appears to have done exactly what he was taught to do. Today I heard that Tiger just had his fourth back surgery. I'm not sure how anyone could ever play golf again after that, much less at the majestic levels he once reached. For your consideration I suggest that our spines were not designed to be used as springs and it might not be desirable to treat them as such.

# AFTERWORD

As I've said, in 2011 I wrote Increase Your Club Head Speed Now. The reason was not that I wanted to get rich – we priced it at $3.95. The reason that I wanted to publish it was to share what I learned with the over-speed training in dramatically increasing my own club head speed after almost fifty years of virtually no gains no matter what swing method or technique of the experts I tried. I was astonished. It worked so well that I shared it with everyone I knew that would listen to me. And it worked with everyone I knew who would try the program for thirty days. To me it was so important that I have summarized it again in the chapter on club head speed in this book. One of the things we noticed when we used the radar device, both me and the other volunteers, is that almost everyone generates extra club head speed with the following counterintuitive swing thought – from the top, whatever you have to do, just get the head of the club on the ball as soon as you can — what traditional golf instruction identifies as casting. Golfers aren't used to trying it, I think, because of the emphasis on "trying" to lag the club head. The interesting thing is that when you video these players intentionally trying to cast it, they never do, at least none that I have seen – their early lag retention is normally fine. I don't claim that it works that way for everybody, but I do know it works for a lot of people, particularly those who you can convince to completely relax their arms. Some of the speed gains from this swing thought can be quite large, five or even more miles per hour. But I didn't say you should cast the club – only, experiment with "trying to" and seeing what result you get when you measure the change, if any. Nothing works for everybody.

Anyway, I sometimes read the reviews that I get on Amazon for the books I have published there. Sorry, I can't help it. I am interested in whether something I have said might help somebody or even whether it didn't. In golf no swing thought helps everybody. One day I came across the following review on Amazon. My small book was rated by Mr. D. Goldbach, given 1 star and titled "would give zero." Verbatim his review was, "this guy didnt teach me anything just told some dumb story about his crapy golf swing and how he gain a few mpgs read the book and came away wishing I didn't. he says casting the club is good, idiot, guess im the idiot for buying it."

Mr. Goldbach, now is my opportunity to respond to your review. I am sorry you had to read about my own golf swing. Unfortunately, speaking about our own experiences is the only way I know to accurately convey information about golf swings. For me to describe what, say Rory was thinking when he hit a drive that carried three hundred-thirty yards would be malarkey. I didn't say to cast the club. I suggested "trying" to cast it and see what result you get. One thing you didn't mention was whether you actually tried the advice. For even one swing. You just assumed I was an idiot – that may be, but now I am an idiot without a distance problem. No, I do not believe you are an idiot for buying the book. But for getting for $3.95 a possible, even likely, solution to a major golf swing issue for yours (buying a book with that title suggests it may be) and not even trying it. Well, that's another matter.

My hope when you finish this book is that you will not be like Mr. Goldbach and assume that because what I have said is outside of the mainstream of standard golf instruction it must be nonsense. The only thing I ask is that you give some of these ideas a try – not for a week or a month, just four or five balls — just long enough to allow your subconscious to get re-oriented.

I do not presume to give golf lessons – I now fully believe that we can only teach ourselves golf. But I would be glad to give you my opinion on any question about the golf swing in which you are interested. We ultimately have to make our journeys alone, but we can at least share our own golf swing conceptions and swing thoughts. You can reach me at tslagle@tds.net. I would like to thank you for purchasing this book and, even more, for reading it to the end. I am quite certain that the present book is the last thing I will write about the golf swing since I no longer wake up in the middle of the night with questions about it.

## MAYBE THE BEST SWING THOUGHT OF ALL

I am born again Christian but I will not try to preach to you. If you are reading this book you have no doubt heard the Gospel of Jesus Christ. But I would like to mention something that occurred to me recently that has changed the way I play golf and live my life in fact. It might sound ridiculous, strange, and absurd but it is no stranger, I believe, than some of the nonsense we try in our own golf swings throughout our lives.

You may remember the little bracelets that some Christians wore back in the seventies that said, "WWJD?" (What Would Jesus Do?). The basic idea was to try to live your life, in whatever you did in your life in the way that Jesus would, if He were in your position. It is really a wonderful idea whether you are a committed Christian or an atheist who believes that Jesus was merely a mythical character. No matter what your belief system modeling your life upon the character of Jesus portrayed in the Bible is admirable.

So I began to wonder. What if this character Jesus were to somehow begin playing golf (even assuming he was not the God-man)? What would his golf game book like? How would he play? How would he practice?

I think he would be a great experimenter. He would try all kinds of different swings and shot shapes. He would work the ball both ways. As far as a swing "method" I do not think he would be a method player or "modeling" player. I seriously doubt that he would try to imitate someone else, even if it were Hogan or Moe or even Count Yogi. I believe he would be the ultimate feel player. He would enjoy every shot he hit, both in play and in practice.

Would he take a traditional golf lesson? Maybe, at least when he first started he might take a brief lesson on traditional grip, stance and posture, but I think after that he would be off on his own lifetime adventure of learning his own golf unique swing. I doubt that he would attend a golf school, read golf magazines or use golf swings aids, unless they were intended to bolster his own God-given hand-eye coordination. I suggest he might be a long hitter since relaxed muscles tend to promote club head speed in virtually everybody.

Perhaps the most interesting thing about playing golf with him is that he would have no interest in the score. A double bogey would be as interesting and enjoyable as an eagle. But without emphasis on the score would that free up his subconscious mind to produce scores on a completely different level? I can imagine a scenario where a playing partner says, "Do you know you just broke the course record?," and he responds: "Really, so what? But we did have a great time, didn't we?" As far as I know no one has ever applied the "WWJD?" concept to their golf swing for a year, a season, a month, a day, or whatever. I think I might play around with it. You might want to play around with it too. It might make you a better player. I am quite sure you will enjoy golf more, maybe much more. It might even help you in other parts of your life.

CPSIA information can be obtained
at www.ICGtesting.com
Printed in the USA
BVOW11s1302210518
516872BV00026B/1203/P